The History of Domestication of Speech

Dr. Kazım Tolga Gürel

Series in Communication

VERNON PRESS

www.vernonpress.com

In the Americas:
Vernon Press
1000 N West Street, Suite 1200
Wilmington, Delaware, 19801
United States

In the rest of the world:
Vernon Press
C/Sancti Espiritu 17,
Malaga, 29006
Spain

Series in Communication

Library of Congress Control Number: 2023950114

ISBN: 979-8-8819-0065-6

Also available: 978-1-64889-818-1 [Hardback]; 978-1-64889-883-9 [PDF, E-Book]

Cover design by Vernon Press. Cover image: 1932 registration: New York herald tribune. Daily, fol. © N. Y. tribune, inc. 6102-6192 v. 91, no. 31093, © Jan. 1, 1932 (B 138766) to v. 91, no. 31182, © Mar. 31 (B 15000S)

Writing is talking about history and the future.

Table of Contents

Abstract

Like all human actions, speaking is one of the most interesting human qualities that have evolved throughout history. Speaking, a concept related to biology, anthropology, sociology, psychology, and politics is also one of the central topics of communication and cultural studies. This study analyses such a profound topic from various perspectives, including its historical evolution and current status. The study's central thesis is that speech has become sterilized with the new sociocultural environment and has lost its revolutionary qualities by becoming compatible with new powers. To strengthen this thesis, the text on the domestication of speech, which many thinkers support, has been created by drawing on history, philosophy, and multidisciplinary sciences on an intense and complex subject.

The question of why the oppression and censorship of speech throughout history has diminished today is answered by linking it to the fact that it has been domesticated and has lost its former power by integrating with the practices of power. The human being is a being who keeps silent as he speaks and postpones one side of the sentence. If it were not for the side that he has postponed and excluded both for himself and his social relations, perhaps order could not be established. Since language and speech, reproduced in conjunction with the practices of power, have lost their revolutionary elements and the ears that would hear speech have been domesticated, a deep scholastic silence continues amidst all this word inflation. Speech has evolved into a counter-revolutionary structure, it has become entirely domesticated, and for this reason, this epoch is characterized by the lowest censorship practices in history. In capital-centered countries, censorship rates have decreased day by day. This is why civilization has reached a structure in which philosophy and analysis have died, and words have lost their meaning and power. Since the structure resembles extensive censorship, visible censorship is no longer needed.

For the last century, speech has been transformed into a commercial product beyond being banned. Power no longer forbids speech; on the contrary, it reproduces it as much as possible and turns it into a commodity. Thanks to communication technologies and big cities, people are no longer silenced, and their silencing slows down the speed of the new cycles of the economy. In such an environment, neither opposing views nor partiality is possible. What appears to be diversity and flavor is essentially very uniform and only a commodity for sale. In this age, speech is domesticated and therefore not censored; on the contrary, silence is forbidden, and silence is madness.

Preface

I have lived in poor neighborhoods in many cities in Turkey. To live in the slums of a third-world country is to live in an abundance of discourse. In places where social rules are looser, far from aristocratic structures, what could be more abundant than the discourse produced by speech? People take refuge in a speech in poverty. Their poverty, impossibilities, problems, and troubles are reflected in speech. The lawlessness of underdevelopment, a chaotic life, and the need to hold on to tradition and each other; in the living spaces of capitalism that produce uncertainty and insecurity, speech becomes an area of comfort and assurance.

I usually sleep with my window open in all seasons, and all the sounds from the street reach inside. Suppose you live with masses of people constantly exploited by the state and kept ignorant by the oligarchy, which comprises all kinds of bureaucrats, soldiers, and bourgeois. In that case, something starts to catch your attention. Especially since the 2000s, when this oligarchy has been accompanied by a twisted peasant revolution and has turned into a one-person regime, that thing that catches your attention becomes much more apparent. People feel the need to talk all the time; this is true for all social classes, but it is as if I have the advantage of experiencing this and witnessing more discourse where I live. Talking is a point of refuge for those far from life's comforts.

I made some bold predictions when I started working on this book in 2013, like thinking that I would finish the book within a year. As I became acquainted with the act of speaking, I realized how profound an activity is and that it is an activity that is influenced by multi-disciplinary knowledge. No matter what I did, something would always need to be added to this work. Speaking was an infinite universe. It was a subject that touched many fields, from linguistics to anthropology, political philosophy to sociology.

Moreover, suppose you live in an anti-democratic state closely related to censorship. In that case, the consciousness of the subjects that make up society is also restricted, and the subject is not independent of politics. It was entirely political. Since it was an endless topic to talk about, I had to stop the book at some point and collect my ideas. Collecting such a broad topic was difficult, and perhaps some points had to remain scattered.

My encounter with an advertisement by a GSM company happened while reading Jorge Louis Borges' *Historia Universal de la Infamia*, in which he mentions that enslaved people were forbidden to talk in the fields. In the advertisement of the GSM company, it was amusingly suggested that the masses speak all the time.

Talking was encouraged and glorified, and the slogan "talk, talk, talk!" was emphasized in the ad. However, Borges' book mentions that enslaved people in the southern states of the United States were punished if they spoke. There were regions and social spaces in history where speech was banned. The process of promoting speech is a historical project.

Why was speech freed by the apparatus of power? Why was it even glorified beyond being freed? Had this speech ceased to be a danger for power? Was it domesticated? Despite being banned in many periods of history and trying to be controlled by pressures imposed primarily on the oppressed class, why is this act subject to inflation strategy today? Why was speech, whose resistive qualities and potential for producing resistance had been recognized in the past, now finding more support at every point? Apart from the commercialization of speech, what factors were involved in this? All these questions form the basic skeleton of this study.

Introduction

Certain areas of the social sciences are doomed to remain at the level of speculation, which is the intuitive power of the social sciences. Intuition has long been excluded from the social sciences because of the harsh rule of positivism. The positivist understanding of science almost broke this intuitive power of the social sciences last century. They imposed on us that speculations are not "facts." But it is impossible to remove intuition from science. Speculation, however, sheds light on reality in a way that still needs to be understood. This intuition brings the social sciences closer to art and gives them creative and philosophical power. If intuitive cognition were to disappear, science, especially social science, would lose much strength, which is why speculation, contrary to what many scientists think, gives social sciences power. Precisely because of these statements, this study will not exclude speculation and does not claim to be "scientific." It aims to reveal a specific process of a phenomenon based on scientific data.

The primary condition for the uprisings of the oppressed to succeed is for people to communicate freely. This is the first condition of being human. But as Rousseau said early on, "Men are born free". But he is everywhere in chains (Rousseau, 2019).

For a long time, when the government's control over people was inadequate, free speech was forbidden in many places. In modern times, however, thanks to a wide range of discourses and practices, from manipulating these reactions to anesthetizing responses and even marketing reactions, reactions are absorbed, produced when necessary, and sold without needing external authority.

Communication has always been challenging for oppressed classes in history. As urban life has developed and the population of the masses has increased, the power of this action has become more evident. As Jean Baudrillard states (1994), the rulers, who saw early on that the masses were not neutral and could take action, realized the power of people in this regard. Byzantine Emperor Iustinianos' banning of gladiatorial and chariot races, which disrupted the discharge mechanisms of society, and riots such as the massive Nika uprising in Constantinople in 532, gave the ruling classes this realization over time (Taddei, 2017). The ruling class's experiences led to increased speech restrictions and censorship of all forms of communication. At that time, the primary condition for the rulers to maintain their sovereignty was to reinforce the static structural elements that could protect the existing structure. For this, they had to tame the "speech" circulating in society.

The word is the way of being of a certain age. It is a reflection of form and a force that directly affects form. The word is not just a simple representation. It is a reality related to change at various levels. Each historical period collects language according to its characteristics and produces it by flexing it according to the formation models of its era. At the same time, speech directly affects every historical process. The speech that circulates in society cannot be considered independent of the individuals and their minds, the general structure of language, and, therefore, the entire material culture that constitutes society's culture. Ultimately, it is tremendously affected by the form of the means of production and the speed of commodity circulation. The word is not independent of the superstructure. The concept transforms more slowly than many others, such as religion, gender, etc. It requires a much longer time for its transformation, and language is transformed due to material practices.

The domestication of the word spread in society means the domestication of the minds of individuals. Therefore, domestication is the only way for governance to maintain its legitimacy. Governance is always capable of dominating discourse. A power that cannot dominate discourse cannot maintain this dominance. When its power starts to break or rupture over discourse, it cracks at every point. Structure, its tools, and governance's first target is existence. Discourse is the fabric of being.

Discourse becomes the fabric of being through the channels of "micro-power." Emotions are integrated into power at the stages of socialization, and no subject can escape it. Countless foci of conflict, points of instability, acts positioned with the criterion of success, beliefs and desires that ground singularities and the internalization of what is constantly acquired through imitation transform the individual into a field of micro-power, and discourse is produced in a way that is built from top to bottom with these networks. Like micro-physical particles, it reflects the power relations scattered in consciousness and the subconscious in the context of a system. It reflects incompletely but ensures performativity and moves the structure in motion. Communication and discourse become the complex voice of the will to power of existence.

So what is discourse? What distinguishes a speech from a sentence? When does a sentence become a discourse, and what turns it into a discourse? How do consumer society and the rapid cycle of commodities affect speech?

Discourse is the recreation of reality through symbols. Discourse is articulating a grammatically structured sentence influenced by human experience and the text. Speech is the production of discourse, not just the production of sentences. Of course, a sentence is a discourse, but not every discourse is a sentence. Through speech, the reality is recreated. By producing discourse, the speaker recreates the event and the experience of the event, which is why saying, "In the beginning was speech," is proof of God. Discourse is not just an event; it is a creation and recreation. A *sentence* is a grammatical string that changes from language to language. It is a tool and soulless. For a sentence to become a discourse, it needs a soul. That soul is the human being with all its historical experience. While communicating, he also visualizes the meaning of every message he tries to convey to the other party in his mind and constructs himself as he speaks. Thus, communicating also means communicating with oneself.

The transformation of language into discourse requires the use of the subject in society. Language existed before the subject and will exist after the subject. Discourse disappears unless it is recorded. It exists within a context or narrative. Language, which is static and fixed, contrasts with discourse, which is dynamic and transforming. Its mobility results from variability and readings in the receiver, the transmitter, and the context.

Discourse can never be neutral; it can never be independent of time and space. Nor can speech be independent of the community; therefore, discourse is never personal. A sentence becomes a discourse from the moment it is read. The Oedipus complex, dazed and ruthlessly repressed by consumer society and the rapid cycle of commodities, generates speech on an enormous scale today.

Discourse produces the subject, and the issue creates the structure. Thanks to the individuals it transforms, the sovereigns and those they keep under sovereignty become subjects in the formation and reproduction of the design with themselves and all their activities. Issues are now ready to be sovereign and to be dominated. The structure will, of course, be changed by human beings when material practices change. However, due to the dialectics of social change, while one group will continue to strive to preserve this structure, another group will want to change it, and it is precisely at this point that Karl Marx explained the social role of the working class. However, the power of the media, the network of brain seduction mentioned by Armand Mattelart, has broken the revolutionary power of the subjects. In the first-world countries mentioned by Herbert Marcuse, the increase in the conditions for the working class to get a share of surplus value has locked them in a prison of a comfortable life. Delusions of gains through political developments, such as social democracy, constitutional rights, etc., have changed the forms of exploitation. The new working conditions brought about by the post Fordist mode of production have eroded this revolutionary side of the working class. The factors that constituted this erosion and revolutionary rupture were reflected in every aspect of communication, and the "word" became domesticated and apolitical, just like the working class. The fact that the personal is political has been subsumed under the painful cries of freedom of individualism. The object of desire that is constantly pursued and the passions that can never be satisfied have led people to envy and emulate each other.

The expanding middle class is encouraged to aspire to the lifestyle of the bourgeoisie, even though they own little property. Hegemony is built on this encouragement. The cheapening of prices through imitation products comes to the rescue of the middle class. Thanks to imitation products, they are included in a similar form to the quality of life of the bourgeoisie. With these lifestyles, many people consume the symbols of the bourgeoisie's culture. This broad middle class, fed on imitations of the material cultural life of the bourgeoisie and the leftovers of the bourgeois lifestyle, makes the rulers' ideology a general atmosphere: social media applications and mass media present slices of their lives. The middle class constantly follows the bourgeoisie and its narratives. The narrative is fiction. However, it dramatically influences both reality and discourse. The middle class, whose discourses are shaped by the narratives of the bourgeois lifestyle, is emasculated in its ability to resist the system. Their dreams, hopes, and even dreams are controlled, the natural causes of the problems of their lives are covered up, and their class position is blurred.

So, how do the masses emulate and imitate the ruling classes' speech patterns, lifestyles, and attitudes? What is the relationship at the core of the flow of messages from the powerful to the powerless, from those who own property to the dispossessed, and from those with status to ordinary people? How does discourse become mass through imitation? To answer these questions, we need to consider Gilles Deleuze's (2023, p. 43) perspective on imitation. Singular blocks of meaning take shape in each subject, and imitation enables the flow. However, this flow is not a flow between equals. Imitation is also subject to a relation of force. According to Deleuze, imitation is an essential element that enables power flow. Power, which is a strategy, operates within relationalities. Power relations are carried within these relationalities. As micro-physics constitutes macro-physics, relationalities also constitute structures.

The subordination of uniqueness to the relationship of power provides a flow due to the relationship of power with lifestyle and money as a matter of the politics of desire. The way of life of the ruling classes is a sign of power for the deprived and subalterns, and they become objects of desire to reach them. Since money and reputation are among the most remarkable objects of desire, they produce imitation. The discourses of money and reputation owners are emulated, internalized, and imitated. Thus, the lifestyles of the ruling classes come to dominate society over time. Antonio Gramsci saw this in the first half of the twentieth century and identified the spread of petty-bourgeois culture.

The spread of petty-bourgeois culture to the broader society is a factor in the decline of the power of resistance to the spoken word. Henceforth, while the apparatuses of power constantly reproduce the word, they also transform individuals into agents for each other through mechanisms that are internalized in the individual. The situation of subjects being "carriers of modes of production," as seen in Poulantzas' ideas (1975), applies here. Like subjects' agency, their discourse is also the result of social causes. Society becomes a collection of subjects who consume domesticated speeches and whose actions often do not match these speeches. Common discourses such as patriotism and nationalism are not enough to unite the subjects diversified by the capitalist way of life. These subjects, who produce discourse rather than labor, cannot satisfy their need for meaning and produce speech rather than production to contribute to life; they seem to want to fill their emptiness with speech.

Word, and therefore speech, contains static and revolutionary elements because it reflects the established reality of society. Material life consists of the dialectical struggle between these two elements. Just as static and kinetic energy can transform into each other, they embody each other as opposites. The fundamental element of communicative action, which constitutes transformation and revolution, must be transformed into a static form, made part of the capitalist market, and positioned as the background force of consumption. Since speech reflects the established reality in the minds, it reproduces this reality ideologically. Through speech, the ideology that dominates society seeps into concrete and abstract concepts. It marginalizes ideas that can constitute constitutive actions and transform the world at the stage of their formation. These revolutionary elements must be included in the glittering world of market products. The glittering world of commodities is also reflected in discourse, sealing the ears against the reality of exploitation. Transitioning from an authoritarian state to a controlling state and then to a new decentralized power that produces discourse is, in fact, the domestication of speech. They are the barriers to establishing a communication structure in which speech can generate revolutionary ideas; thanks to these barriers, life is organized through the reality of exploitation.

Chapter 1

The Conversation is Born

Shadow: I have not listened to you speak for a long time; I would like to make it easier for you to speak.

Traveler: Someone is speaking - where is he? Who is it? He is so close to me that he says, 'It is I who speak'; yet his voice sounds weaker than mine.

Shadow (after a while): 'Aren't you glad you have found a way to speak?'

Traveler: I swear by God, whom I do not believe, and by all beings, that it is my shadow that speaks; I hear it speak, but I do not believe it.

Friedrich Nietzsche (2022, p. 5)

Thousands of definitions have been made about human beings. Legends and religious texts first defined this infinite and unknowable being; works of art and philosophical texts of the same period expanded this definition. Recent scientific studies have buried this unknowability in even more robust agnosticism, contrary to popular belief. Even fields such as physiology, endocrinology, and hematology are pregnant with discoveries. These are fields that continue to be studied. Despite being thought to be explained with certainty in the past, scientific studies, albeit by the light of a candle, have enlightened the concept of the "human being," which is religious mysticism resulting from the unknowability of humans and the universe they perceive. However, it remains hidden in the darkness. Although science, which Paul Feyerabend calls the "new tradition," has shed new light on the concept of the human being, it has not gone beyond a small step since its existence is multi-perspective and infinite.

Many thinkers have tried to define human beings from their perspectives, using names such as "Zoon Politikon," "Homo Faber," "Homo Ludens," "Homo Loquens," and "Homo Economicus." However, when we think about these expressions, we see that they all remain within a narrow framework or draw a boundary that can confuse humans with other living beings. These definitions deal with an infinite being from one or a few perspectives. Since the subject of this study is "speech," this study will also look at it from one perspective. Ernest Cassirer's conceptualization of human beings, which is the most realistic and determines the top quality that distinguishes them from all living things, is Ernest Cassirer's "Homo Symbolicum." All living things speak, including trees.

The structures of the speech of other living things are entirely different. As for humans, the air is not their primary determinant. In his work "An Essay on Man," this German philosopher, who defines humans as a species that uses symbolic tools, identifies the top quality that distinguishes him from other living beings as the use of symbolic tools. Humans are animals that evolved their socialization by using symbols.

Ernst Cassirer states that the question of the origin of language must be as old as the question of the origin of the perception of being. Because he says that the first conscious reflection of human beings can be realized through language, he associates words and meaning with the perception of the object and the process of the subject becoming a subject himself. Cassirer emphasizes that the world of language surrounds human beings. In the relationship between language and existence, he refers to the constitutive effect of language on existence: Language, too, first existed with a remarkable indifference in the face of the division of the world into two distinct spheres, the 'inner' and the 'outer' spheres of being. The language was formed before the world of perception was divided into two, which is part of the essence of language. Spiritual content and its sensory expression appear here so embedded in each other that one does not exist before the other as independent and self-sufficient. Instead, it is first completed in the spiritual content. Both expression and content first become what they are in mutual penetration. As they relate, meaning is not only added to their being from the outside. Moreover, this meaning becomes, first of all, what constitutes this being (Cassirer, 2005, p. 162).

The animal identifies directly with its vital activity. It does not separate itself from it. In other words, it is this activity. Will and consciousness are directed toward humans' vigorous exercise. Humans have a conscious vital activity. Humans are not a determination with which it is directly fused. A conscious critical activity instantly distinguishes humans from the essential movement of the animal. It is precisely because of this, and only because of this, that humans are unique beings. Or humans are conscious beings only because they are sexual beings; in other words, their own lives are an object for them. Its activity is free only because of this (Marx, 2007, p. 27).

Since the last half-century, studies have shown that humans are not the only ones capable of learning. What distinguishes human beings from other living beings is not the ability to learn but the necessity to learn. The need to learn is linked to the fact that, like other living beings, humans lack instincts that directly direct their lives. While other animals are armed with instincts embedded in their genes, humans have to act by forming social organizations, and the primary tool of this organization is language. One of the most critical aspects of human evolution and survival is the ability to speak.

Of course, human spoken language is closely related to the ability to control the muscles of the mouth and larynx. On the other hand, sign language is about controlling facial muscles and expressing this to another person through gestures and facial expressions. Human spoken language evolved from sign language, which consists of gestures and facial expressions (Spiteri et al., 2007). For example, sign language-based communication in autistic children can be acquired before speech is shown evidence (Stokoe, 1978, p. 5; Hunt-Jackson, 2007). In other words, visual communication based on sign language emerged before vocal communication. The most significant proof of this is the existence of mirror neurons. Mirror neurons were first discovered in the frontal cortex of the monkey brain. They are called mirror neurons because when a monkey acts, similar neurons fire in the brain of the other monkey as if it were performing the same action, and the behavior is reflected (Fitch, 2005).

The new findings on the FOXP2 gene in humans align with other findings on the anatomical emergence of modern humans (homo sapience). Estimates that everyday speech dates back to around 150,000–200,000 years ago are strengthened by the results of FOXP2 research, although they are still inconclusive. There are different views on this issue. Some think Neanderthals could not speak; they think they had limited speech, and those think they had language or languages similar to ours.

Although it is not yet known which species spoke first, the evidence that these species contributed to the evolution of speech is getting stronger daily. The hyoid bone, language-related brain regions, the position of the larynx, and FOXP2 genes have strengthened the possibility that Neanderthals also spoke (Kerimoğlu, 2022). The fact that these species lived in herds makes the argument that there was communication between them very clear. However, is this a communication speech? "If it is speech, is it as advanced as today's languages?" These and similar questions continue to be researched.

John Zerzan, quoting many anthropologists, also concludes in his famous study "Future Primitive" that it is almost sure that Homo habilis possessed the central human mental and communicative abilities. According to Zerzan, the idea that the human mind was backward in the past compared to its present counterparts is a myth-symbolic culture results from a need, not a development (Zerzan, 2004).

One of the language's most important features is that it binds the subjects who speak that language together. As a result of this interconnectedness, social rules are formed. By its very nature, co-existence produces a sense of repression in each subject. The human ability to communicate includes, on the one hand, knowledge of language use and, on the other hand, the traditionalized extra-linguistic features that apply to every speech community. These extra-linguistic features derive from the many deeper qualities of geography-matter-human relations and affect speech. In this sense, the use of language is much more than grammar. Each subject is embedded in its discourse.

Even though theories about the formation of language are rooted in the founding fathers of philosophical idealism and can be treated with concepts such as "logos" and Sophist inquiry into speech, they were studied for the first time in the eighteenth century. Wilhelm Humboldt was the first thinker to analyze the effect of language on the formation of consciousness. He stated that human beings become human only through language and considered language as one of the foundations of the human being.

According to Humboldt, there are two constructive principles in language: the inner language-sense (inere Sprachsinn) – by this, Humboldt means all the mental faculties involved in the use and development of language. The inner language sense is the principle that dominates language from within, that gives everything a driving impulse. Sound could have remained equal to passive, form-giving matter, but with the sense of language, it has become the creative principle in language, encompassing thought and the senses. The internal language sense is equal in every language. On the other hand, sound is the principle that increases differences (Akarsu, 1998, p. 25).

Humboldt was wrong when he said that every language's internal language sense is equal. What is equal are hormonal emotions such as fear, anger, and love. However, culture comes into play as soon as the feeling forms. We cannot speak of a language sense that is equal for all people. What all people have is the ability to learn a language.

It is known that the first form of communication was non-verbal. Before becoming human beings, people spoke with their bodies and faces. In his research in 1872, Charles Darwin revealed that certain expressions of the face are universal. He showed that some words are unlearned and common to other mammals (Tubbs and Moss, 2003, p. 118). At the social level, men and women learn their body language during their development, and this dualism is strictly social, not biological. One of the most fundamental aspects of gendering is the way of speaking. Male and female communication is structured and differentiated by gender. The thinness and thickness of the voice are natural, but gestures, vocalizations, and the structure of discourse are gendered. While personal qualities are acquired through genes, imitation, etc., the postures given to them by society are also articulated over time, and each subject receives a verbal and non-verbal communication vocabulary. Since there was no distinction between men and women in early human societies since gender had not yet emerged, there was no such distinction. It can be argued that nonverbal communication was genderless at that time. Today, however, patriarchal societies have given nonverbal communication a gendered structure.

Another form of non-verbal communication encompasses dance, music, painting, sculpture, and architecture. All these arts are as old as humanity. The oldest musical instrument is the flute, which is thought to have been made about 40,000–70,000 years before the speech. Symbols made with bones found around 30,000 years ago are another example of non-verbal communication (Rosengren, 2008, p. 40).

What can be understood from the sentence "Language is a double-layered prison?" A person is a prisoner of apriori symbols because of the language. That is the first layer from which one can never get out. But there is another layer, which is caused by class societies. The way of life of class society burdens and constructs a person in such a way that this construction leads to the second layer of the prison.

The oppression in class societies has divided people into being inside and outside. This is the giant trap that civilization has set. As humans began to realize themselves in the last 250–100 thousand years, they entered this prison. As civilization has become more complex, the conviction to keep thoughts and feelings inside has also increased. Today's humans are the most talkative species in their evolutionary chain, with the greatest need to assert themselves. Speech is different from the communication of other animals. It is different because it is a means of self-existence and questioning the world beyond the physical needs of humans. By speaking, humans first prove their existence to themselves. Proving oneself to oneself may make one question the following point: As alienation increases, does the need to talk also increase?

Even today, many people still refuse to accept the facts about evolution, even though ideas about the origin of human beings began to break out of religious beliefs and mythology from the time of ancient Greek thinkers. Many of the world's population still believe in religious mythology and descent from Adam and Eve. Before we begin to explain the facts about the origin of beings, it is necessary to illustrate some of these beliefs. Islam, Christianity, and the Torah support the Adam and Eve mythology. This is natural, given their period. It is interesting that millions of people today still need to believe it. However, a few observations can shed light on this issue in a world where COVID-19 is evolving in front of everyone's eyes. Many still think that archaeological findings and "skull hunting support the theory of evolution."

An English priest named James Ussher, who, at the beginning of the eighteenth century, had concluded that the first skulls found in the early eighteenth century were 6,000 years old and that "the creation of man must have been 4,004 B.C." was supported by religious books. James Ussher should not be too surprised. Harun Yahya, who lives in the Republic of Turkey today, goes even further and claims to have disproved the theory of evolution and bases his evidence on distorted interpretations of religion. Moreover, there are a significant number of people who believe what this Harun Yahya says. More interestingly, since he is a capitalist, he has been spreading anti-evolution propaganda for a long time by distributing his books printed on glossy paper and through the television he owns. Today, in many countries, such innocent-looking people believe in a paradigm other than the scientific one. Nevertheless, these religious people in the past burned Galileo Galilei and skinned the Islamic dervish Hallaci Mansur to death.

Originating 70 million years ago, when the first primates separated from semi-apes, humanization has its historical-biological origins. Within this development process, the first humanoid apes and Hominids began to emerge around 25–30 million years ago (Teber, 2018, p. 55). Although no exact time can be given, some species living in Africa began to show humanoid characteristics around 5 million years ago. It is estimated that the herds of the period consisted of 50–150 humans. According to Harari (2015), the memory capacity of the human mind today is still limited to this number. The number of people we know directly, without any communication, is at most 150; this is our brain's capacity from an archaic way of life.

Human evolution is a complex structure resulting from biological and cultural interactions. There are no sharp transitions in this evolution; there are transitional periods and species. Changes occurred in different periods on every continent. Evolution is a prolonged process that takes place over millions of years. Charles Darwin (1809–1882) laid the foundations of the theory of evolution. Darwin argued that all species evolved from a single species or group of species through natural selection. He supported his views with much evidence according to the conditions of the time. The scientific world accepted the theory in the 1930s. This theory, the most logical explanation of the diversity of life ever put forward, was developed much further after Darwin and supported by different branches of science. Darwin's particular achievement was to arrive at a plausible hypothesis about how organisms change to become more adapted to their immediate environment. According to his theory, the following propositions are true:

There are many individual differences within an animal or plant population.

At least some of these are inherited from one generation to the next.

Within a given generation, more individuals reproduce than can survive by reproduction.

Some differences are likely to persist more than others depending on the environment in which they live. They will reproduce themselves more than others. (Benton and Craib, 2008, p. 62).

The dating of evolution has advanced considerably with scientific advances since Charles Darwin. In Darwin's time, the age of the earth was thought to be around 100 million years. However, geophysics and geological science advances have strengthened our understanding of evolution. Although their reliability has decreased, some techniques include stratigraphic correlations, fluoride absorption analysis, potassium argon technique, and the carbon 14 method. Radiometric techniques such as TL and ESR are beyond the scope of this study. However, it should be known that unreachable temporal processes can be reached thanks to these techniques. In this sense, with the contribution of developments in other sciences, the evolutionary process is becoming increasingly enlightened daily. There are still significant areas for improvement in terms of historical accuracy. However, the lack of historical certainty does not mean its chain development is not illuminated.

When the Adam and Eve story began to be shaken, the first fossil human skull was found in Gibraltar in 1848 but did not receive the attention it deserved. The head of a Neanderthal man found in Düsseldorf, Germany, in 1856 was one of the first revolutionary findings in this field (Teber, 2004, p. 42). The name of the group that includes humans is a primate, and this covers species such as chimpanzees, humans, gorillas, etc., with their colloquial names. The word primate was first used by the Swedish naturalist Linne. All primates, highly diverse in morphological, physiological, biochemical, and behavioral patterns, are lumped together without distinction under a wildly inaccurate word called ape. This word has no scientific meaning, leading to misunderstandings (Özbek, 2000, p. 44).

The geological timeline is divided into the Archaean, First Time, Second Time, Third Time, and Fourth Time. Mammals existed on Earth during the Third Time and the Fourth Time. Among primates, the period in which hominids diverged from the others is called "Miocene," a division within the Third Time. It is estimated that this divergence took place around 10 million years ago. But what caused this divergence?

Some 40–50 million years ago, small-bodied, long-tailed monkeys could live a reasonably secure life on high trees in tropical forests among abundant plant foods. Towards the middle of the third geoscientific period, these little monkeys finally had to put their feet on the ground as the woods began to diminish. A new life full of various fears and possibilities began for them (Teber, 2004, p. 153). These fears led them to accelerate the development of their communicative processes and to become more socialized. Since primates living in natural conditions today can distinguish between many sounds, communicate with each other, and communicate danger to other colony members, these creatures, whose habitats have changed with the decline of forests, tend to increase their communicative qualities.

If one were to travel to Africa 7 million years ago to observe the behavior of early humans, one would find a pattern that would be more familiar to primatologists who study the behavior of apes and hominids than anthropologists who study the behavior of humans. Rather than living in family communities in migratory groups like hunter-gatherers, early humans probably lived more like savanna baboons (Abyssinian monkeys). Groups of about thirty individuals coordinated foraging over a wide area and returned to suitable sleeping places, such as hills or clusters of trees at night. Most of the group consisted of adult females and their children, with only a few adult males. Males were constantly seeking mating opportunities, and dominant individuals were more successful. Males who had not reached adulthood or were at a low level were only on the group's periphery and hunted for food independently. The group's individuals were human-like in bipedal walking but behaved like savanna primates. They had 7 million years of evolution ahead of them, which, as we will see, was highly complex and imprecise. Natural selection works according to immediate circumstances, not towards a long-term goal. Homo Sapiens eventually emerged as the descendant of the first humans, but this was by no means an inevitable development (Leakey, 1993).

Today, it is known that there was communication between these species, who were not very different from us physically. The fact that they were organized, hunted, and met many of their needs indicates strong communication ties between these people. In particular, it is known that they made tools collectively, which can only happen with speech and communication.

While all these developments were taking place, language was progressing along with them, influencing and being influenced by them. While some linguists theorized on language formation, others theorized on human speech perception. Edward Saphir and Benjamin Lee Whorf, who lived at different times, are among these thinkers. According to the hypothesis that came to be known as the Saphir-Whorf hypothesis, languages cause speakers of that language to think in specific ways. This is why the vocabulary of desert Bedouins about desert sand is more significant than that of English. Therefore, they can produce more ideas about desert sand and talk about the functions of these objects in a richer language.

Language influences perceptual processes and enables certain types and thoughts to be easily expressed. However, language cannot ultimately determine the content of the idea; if there is an actual perceptual event and this event must be told in words, the thought creates a new comment, a concept and finds the expression of the new idea (Cüceloğlu, 2020, p. 214).

Human fossils exemplify archaic Homo Sapiens communities from the Boxgrove quarry in Sussex. Judging from their tools, mainly handaxes, scrapers, and spearheads, it is clear that they had switched from scavenging to hunting.

About half a million years ago, four rhinos were hunted here, each yielding 700kg of meat. There are interpretations that the hunt had to be planned, so talking was necessary. Its erect forehead and 1,100–1,400 cubic centimeters of brain support these interpretations (Şenel, 2009, p. 86).

The hunt of four rhinos requires a much more complex communication than the signaling language of involuntary screams caused by muscle tension in fear. Such a hunt is unlikely without a monosyllabic form of communication but one that is relatively independent of reflexive signals. A family of lions armed with a much more diverse set of prey organs might be able to do it, but for humans, the weapon of choice is communication and a well-developed brain that enables it.

Human history covers 90% of the Paleolithic era. Humans have only recently developed into what they are today. The middle Paleolithic period covers a period of 250 thousand years on average. When all these processes are considered, it will be understood that the period of 6 thousand years called history is short. Homo Sapiens, the original ancestors, is known to encompass various human races. Despite all the findings, these periods are still the cradle of many life forms that remain dark. What is clear is that communication between humans has always been abundant and has existed since the beginning. Humans have always been talking beings.

It is almost impossible to imagine, with modern consciousness, the human being that existed during the evolution of Homo Sapiens. That of modern times, almost completely detached from nature and striving to control it, cannot or does not want to think of its ancestors in that state. Thanks to monotheistic religions and the glorification of the myth of the individual, the building block of bourgeois society, today we think we are God. Masters of the universe in our delusion. The fact that humans are primates and that humans' ancestors were ape-like creatures that have been despised for centuries weighs heavily on many. However, anthropology establishes this fact with more and more solid evidence daily.

The causes of primate diversity are a hotly debated topic in anthropology. Primates have diversified due to their adaptation to different ecological niches. Some primates are active during the day, others at night. Some eat insects, others fruit, shoots, leaves, digestive plants, seeds, and roots. The rest are omnivores. Some primates live on the ground, others in trees, and there are species with intermediate forms. However, because the earliest primates lived in trees, modern primates share similarities that reflect their ancestral heritage of tree life (Kottak, 2008, p. 145). These qualities of primates are inferred from the similarities of the present. Evolutionary periods have been clarified in line with efforts to make sense of the past through various mediations. However, of course, efforts to explain evolution are not only through mediation.

Thanks to fossils, Stone Age tools, and recent molecular genetics, it is clear that modern humans, which have been evolving for 100,000 years, originated from an African community that lived around 200,000 years ago. From there, these people dispersed to other parts of the world. It has been assumed that they evolved differently in varying regions, but this does not make sense and is contrary to the molecular data. When a new species arrives in a new habitat, its flexibility gives it an advantage over other species in the region. Within certain limits, it is also possible that interspecific matings contribute to regional continuity. However, suppose the African case is taken as a whole. In that case, the emergence of modern humans' dates back to 100,000 years ago, and this would be the most appropriate and reliable starting point to begin understanding the human journey (Cowen, 2004, p. 27).

As hunters and gatherers, Erectus are highly adaptable creatures compared to their predecessors. Although not accepted by some anthropologists, the fact that they hunted en masse strengthens the fact that there was communication between them. The fact that they have a brain similar in size to Homo Sapiens also supports the argument that they communicate.

Anthropological evidence confirms that they hunted large animals cooperatively and were able to produce complex tools. These activities are too complex to be carried out without some language. Speech helps with coordination, cooperation, learning customs, and even tool-making. Words, of course, were preserved in the advent of writing. However, given the potential for language-based communication – which even chimpanzees and gorillas share with Homo sapiens – and a capacity within the lower limits of Homo sapiens' brain size, it seems reasonable to assume that Homo erectus was able to speak, albeit in a primitive manner (Kottak, 2008, p. 210).

Around 100,000 years ago, our earliest ancestors communicated through wordless gestures and an evolving spoken language system. As their lives became more and more complex, they needed more than the group's collective memory to remember essential things. They required a memory outside the body, sometimes called extra somatic memory. Thus, the increase in 'communication' led to the emergence of 'means of communication' and tools to store the increasing volume of data and retrieve it when needed (Crowley and Heyer, 2017, p. 18). The brain is at a point where it can no longer carry social messages, and the evolution of society has expanded the number of social news.

The transferability of knowledge is one of the most apparent reasons for the evolution of the human species up to the present day. Other species also pass on knowledge to the next generation, but this knowledge is limited. Compared to humans, other primates die without passing on knowledge to their offspring. Humans leave twenty million years of knowledge to their offspring. Language has given humans rapid development, making them far superior to other living beings. Since humans started using language, a new dialectic began to take place. This dialectic is the language-thought dialectic. Freedom is realized through his language. The dependence of thought on language has been demonstrated. The first to think was the first to speak (Hançerlioğlu, 1977, p. 15). Language, the transmission of thought, is created by labor itself. We can see this among other predatory animals that rely on teamwork rather than brute force or speed to kill their prey. They have a series of hunting commands and warnings - the beginnings of language (Brooks and Pickard, 2012, p. 73).

The brain structure of Stone Age people was highly developed due to tens of thousands of years of tool-making by previous evolutionary cycles. Although the existence of a simple speech center is debated in science, the dialectic of production inevitably developed thought and speech centers. The main factor that developed this ability is that the early stages of the evolutionary chain were adapted to work and were forced to communicate due to environmental conditions. With a face and body structure adapted to the ice age, Neanderthals were the first species to wear clothes. They were able to hunt reindeer, mammoths, and woolly rhinoceroses with much better-crafted tools and were better adapted than Homo Erectus, which is likely the result of communication.

Due to the cold climate, they have different facial features. They developed a unique morphology and reached their most advanced state at the beginning of the last glacial period (-75000 years). Neanderthals are found throughout Europe and the Middle East (Özbudun, Uysal, Duran, 1998, p. 29). They could live during the glacial period by humidifying the air with a long, wide nose. In addition, their torsos are developed, and their arms and legs are shorter. The "Neanderthal," whose hands and brains differentiated from other primates due to manual labor, lived approximately 100 thousand years ago and most likely had a common language because they worked together and collaborated with their peers. Here is what Soviet anthropologists Ilin and Segal have to say about the speech of this evolutionary circle, which had to get along because of how they lived, even though the area under the jaw differed from today's humans: How did humans communicate? With the whole body. Since no particular speech organs were yet as developed as they are today, the whole body spoke: the muscles of the face, the shoulders, the feet, and the hands (Illin and Segal, 2016, p. 21). Gestures, i.e., body language, is the oldest human language. Even though the communication during this period was an impulsive communication intensity that depended on the motor-nerve center, there was a very high probability of communication in Neanderthals.

Knowledge about the communication of present-day primates is necessary to illuminate the period. Chimpanzees greet each other with gestures, facial expressions, and screams and make owl-like calls to maintain contact throughout their daily encounters (Kottak, 2008, p. 154). Gombe chimpanzees use 25 different screams. Each has a distinct meaning and is used only in specific situations. Because screams are automatic and cannot be combined, language is more flexible. Primates can only simultaneously make a single sound when confronted with food and danger. They cannot combine their cries for food and danger into a single utterance that expresses the presence of both. Even if they can do so by chance, others do not understand it (Kottak, 2008, p. 158).

The concept of "I," which is a historical project, must develop to move on to known human communication. The individuals must abstract their existence from nature and society, just as children realize their existence and become independent from the progenitor, as detailed in Piaget's and Lacan's teachings. In the first forms of speech, in which body language was dominant in communication, human beings were not yet rich in "abstraction" at this point in social evolution. There is much abstraction in today's language, but language represented more material phenomena back then.

The harsh conditions during the Neanderthal period, the development of culture over time, the increase in experience, and the division of labor made body language inadequate, and monosyllabic sounds were added to these languages tens of thousands of years old. Neanderthal's speech and vocalizations are due to the need to frighten other creatures, satisfy the most fundamental instincts, and coordinate due to the lack of organization to meet these instincts. The Neanderthal spoke more intensely than other evolutionary rings due to the difficult living conditions, which indicates how much human speech depends on external conditions in every period. Archaeologist Steven Mithen describes the living conditions of Neanderthals as follows:

> At first glance, in this diversity of prey animals, it may seem that Neanderthals lived in a Garden of Eden. But the reality is very different. Putting together the necessities of life – food, shelter, warmth – must have been highly challenging to Neanderthals. Just because animal and plant resources are diverse does not mean they are abundant. Each animal depends on a vegetation cover, leading to frequent and unpredictable fluctuations in the number of animals. Frequent environmental changes caused by the advance or retreat of ice sheets or just a few years of relative cooling or warming continue. This means that food cover composition and relationships are constantly changing. (Mithen, 2000, p. 145)

Homo Neanderthals constituted one of the essential evolutionary leap periods in human history, not only with their remote hunting methods but also with the methods of vocal communication, speech, and, to a lesser extent, abstraction that they undoubtedly developed conditionally. Again, within this developmental process, for the first time, within the increasingly intensified and active social consciousness, the fields of religious and artistic consciousness gradually began to produce their unique products. Homo Neanderthals were the first ancestors in human history to bury their dead ceremoniously. In grave findings, skeletal remains of the dead were found, painted with red ochre, in sitting or lying positions, sometimes adorned with various ornaments and jewelry, and sometimes even buried with the items they used in their daily lives (Teber, 2018, p. 70).

As seen in the development of Neanderthal's technologies, their culture's struggle for survival led to an explosion. Language also took its share of this explosion. Improved hunting also led to improved communication between them. The most fundamental consequence of the imbalance in vegetation – the main factor in this was the glacial periods – was the development of Neanderthal hunting and hunting organizations, which would have meant an increase in their power of communication. Anthropologist Randall White highlights seven pieces of archaeological evidence that point to dramatic advances in linguistic abilities in the Upper Paleolithic:

> First, the tradition of conscious burial, which began with the Neanderthals but developed only in the Upper Palaeolithic (with the practice of burying the dead with their belongings); second, artistic expressions in the form of imagery and bodily ornamentation, which began only in the Upper Palaeolithic and Late Stone Age; third, the sudden acceleration in the pace of cultural change due to technological innovations; fourth, the first fundamental regional differences in cultural development, reflected as a symptom and product of social boundaries; fifth, strong evidence of contacts with distant localities and the exchange of foreign objects between groups; sixth, a significant expansion of living space (complex language became a prerequisite for planning and coordination); seventh, a shift from a technology fundamentally dependent on stone as a raw material to other materials such as bone, antler, and clay. (Lewin, 2004, p. 212)

It remains unknown how Neanderthals moved from a monosyllabic language supported by body language to a complex language, that is, due to which structures the signifier-signified relationship was established. The signifier-signified property makes linguistic signs both causeless and linear. The linguistic sign is causeless because the signifier (concept) is bound to the signified (auditory image) in a numerical, consensual manner; this bond is not natural but social. The signifier is a social and psychic self that arises not from the individual's free act of realization but from the linguistic system. On the other hand, the orality of the signifier is realized in the flow of time, which makes the sign linear. This feature gives the system of signs called language a privilege among other methods of characters (Rıfat, 1990, p. 17).

Words carry thoughts on their backs and serve to create them. Words are magical processors that help to mesmerize people. They transmit thoughts and things to others and melt into each other, acquiring other meanings in an ascending spiral. Words have their life span; they, too, are mortal. Language enables human beings to think and create the agent and even think with the agent (Baudrillard, 2005, p. 14). Thought attached to language cannot be individual; it goes back and forth between us and the world. It is necessary to say that the human shapes the world (Baudrillard, 2005, p. 97).

What one person says with one word is not the same as what another person says with another, and every difference, no matter how small, spreads throughout the language like a ring in water. That is why every understanding is a non-understanding; every unification of thought and feeling is also a separation. Humans are not transparent even to themselves and for themselves (Chul Han, 2023, p. 17).

Human beings have started to live in a narrative universe from the moment they became human, and this is one of the most fundamental characteristics of the community they form. The human community constantly produces narratives. These narratives are not limited to language and speech. Every element that constitutes culture is an element of a particular narrative string and is itself directly a narrative. In a sense, culture is the articulation of narratives. Roland Barthes expresses this situation as follows:

> There are too many narratives in the world to count. Above all, there are an astonishing number of genres. These genres, in turn, are scattered across different entities, as if every object is suitable for human beings to trust and open their narratives. The basis of history can be spoken language (spoken or written), image (static or dynamic), gesture, and a regular mixture of these elements. (Barthes, 1988, p. 7)

Humans must live in a community, and speech arose as a result. Spoken language (*language articulé*) is formed and developed during work. Thought, human consciousness, is endowed with the faculty of abstraction; in other words, human beings can reflect and synthesize the reality surrounding thought and consciousness into concepts that can be expressed in words. This faculty of abstraction has enabled human beings to express their thoughts and feelings in words; language, on the other hand, has made it possible to exchange information in the bosom of society. But this possibility alone is insufficient for the emergence of organized speech. For this reason, the transmission of ideas to others must, first of all, be prescriptive. (...) Work has always been a social phenomenon. The efforts of a single individual have formed an integral part of the life of an entire community. Community members collaborating for work has led the individual to regard himself as part of the community, to submit to its requirements, and to consider himself only as a member. Because of this joint work, people felt the need to communicate and speak (Zubritski, Mitropolski, and Kerov, 2012, p. 16). One of the theories of the origin of language is the "onomatopoeic" (phonetic) theory, which argues that language was born by imitating the sounds of nature. Such a view may not cover the whole reality of language. But there is no doubt that voice mimicry played an essential role in creating words (vowel symbols). Words and phrases such as "civ civ" and "woof woof" persist in our language even today and are proof of this. Their proportion must have been much higher during the formation of primitive language, meaning that symbols are (in some respects) similar to objects (Şenel, 2009).

When people lived in small communities, their communication was limited. This is because it was often only through warfare that they had the opportunity to meet, which is why languages developed in different structures. In addition, the first human groups of 100–150 people were relatively isolated. Isolation is necessary for a spoken language to develop. For speech to evolve into a different language, two groups of people must not come into contact with each other. Geographical conditions are one of the most important reasons for this isolation. Since the human population was not very large in the early times, many groups did not meet each other. In short, this isolation required for the formation of languages arose for three main reasons: geographical separation, lack of encounter due to lack of population, and conflicts with each other.

According to Mario Pei (1960), if two groups are formed by building a barrier between the eastern and western parts of the United States, and if these two groups do not communicate for ten years, they will have difficulty understanding each other after a while. Pei's claim of ten years is debatable, but the common language will inevitably diverge after a certain period.

Each of the human communities with poor communication with each other has developed its unique communication system, and these communication systems have started to evolve within themselves. Culture has been passed down from generation to generation thanks to speech. They have preserved their work habits, formed their cultural character, and taught these cultures to the next generations. From an anthropological point of view, language comes before art and religion. These begin at a time when humans can situate themselves to some extent apart from nature and the other members of their species. Humans have to make sense of the reasons for their and nature's existence. There is now a certain level of sophistication in the ability to describe, leading to a desire to attribute specific causes to his cultural attributes. But language, although it contains the ability to explain to some extent, is born of reflexive movements of the nervous motor system. Language, therefore, exists before consciousness and reason. The communication apparatus in animals is the most basic proof of this, which is why the birth of a communication apparatus predates the formation of art and religion.

Ignorance or different information about dreams and death, plus the fact that some of the material phenomena around them acted like living beings (fire, sea, etc.), gave rise to the idea that each being had a soul. The dream was perceived and considered accurate, just like the material world. The difference between life and death became blurry as reality was confused with the dream. Therefore, there is no sharp line between life and death. Their ancestors continue to live with them, sometimes as a spirit, tree, or squirrel. That is why they talk to trees and other living things and have the utmost respect for nature. Because they cannot objectify nature, nature is identical to their culture. Nature is their ancestor and family with whom they talk and communicate. It is a relative for them. This perfect unity is not a form of communication that other consciousness can easily understand.

By developing funeral rites, spells, and magic, humanity communicated with nature and strengthened this communication through various narratives, rituals, and religious, artistic, and magical elements. These communications gave rise to the first ideological structures seen in savage societies, and the thought clusters that reconstructed reality began to be molded. These would become so powerful that they would continue as concepts such as magic and evil eye in our life practices and various religions. These are phenomena left over from our previous way of communicating with existence. These powerful phenomena are the interactive realities of that period.

It is difficult to understand such a perception of nature since, today, the relationship is based on possession and exploitation. It is almost impossible to empathize because there is a massive difference between this grammar of being and today's grammar regarding the human being. It is precisely for this reason that the discourse of some cultures did not remain outside them. This discourse is already the spirit and directly touches the physical body, which is the most powerful suggestion dimension. Because it is the moment when the word is directly material, but what is material is also a complete spirit. The word is not external and alien to the human being; instead, it is directly an organ of the human being. It has power, like breath, because it is not outside him. In all rituals, the relationship with being is poetry and art. At that time, there was no distinction between matter and metaphysics. The word interacts with matter; this is precisely why the word "dua" in the Qur'an means "word" in ancient Arabic, and "ruh" means breath.

In an oral culture, where the word exists only in the form of sound, referring to no visually perceptible text of any kind, the phenomenology of the word is very much implicated in the human sense of being, processed by speech. How discourse is experienced always occupies an essential place in psychic life. The centralizing efficacy of sound (the field of sound is not scattered in front of the human being, but instead, it is all-encompassing) affects the human sense of the cosmos (Crowley and Heyer, 2017, p. 113).

The sound emitted by speech produces the illusion that the human being is at the center. A person's relationship with their voice places them at the center of the world when they speak. Voice surrounds all around. However, the delusion of being at the center is also related to the construction of the self. It may be true for current human beings, but not when there wasn't a central ego.

In a ritual, speech sounds can be understood as the sounds of the universe, and people lose themselves in this energy. This multiplicity develops an ambiance that encompasses the whole universe with the group ritual and the sounds of nature. The poetic sound of speech pervades the whole body and the whole being.

The first organization of primitive people was around the clan. The clan believes that it is under the sacred protection of a higher being. This being is the absolute protector of people and property; it is usually symbolized in an animal and becomes the sign of the clan, the totem, because of its divine power. This totem possesses all life resources and uses them as it pleases. A council of elders ruled the clan for a long time. Authority is widespread and dispersed (Ateş, 2021, p. 16). How did this dispersed authority come to be concentrated in the hands of a chief and become the right of a single person? Although there is no definitive answer to this question, many theories exist. However, in any case, this power structure will initially be based on word of mouth.

Chapter 2

Power Based on Speech

The organizer/rule-maker is subject to the same social power when everything a human being has is carried in their body and is limited to a small space. In a ritual, the word appears from the outside to be the word of the shaman, but in reality, it is the word of the whole being. The shaman who speaks in ritual is an apparatus, an instrument of Mana. Mana is the power that permeates all beings and actions. People who speak are listened to, not because of their wealth but because of their experience. The one with experience has power, but this power is not used to exploit another. It is well known that exploitation will plague the clan, just as violence. As Girard (2019) emphasizes, violence is ended with sacrificial rituals. The resentment that causes violence can be transferred to the sacrificed object and buried with it, just as power is poured into nature, which is viewed as supreme.

In almost every society, speech is a sign of power. The most obvious proof of this assertion is that in every community, there are people who have a voice and people who do not. The hierarchy in class societies ensures that some people have a stronger voice and others are excluded. Considering the difference between the word of head of state and the word a "madman" - a difference that is related to historical change and the norms of society - it can be seen that the discourse of the "madman" is marginalized or that the address of those who hold power in their hands is powerful because they have a strong sanction. This disparity between discourses also indicates that speech is a powerful energy carrier.

Words gain functionality and value only when they are repeatable. Words that cannot be easily uttered and repeated are transformed or disappear. However, some words are subjected to efforts to eradicate them through repression and censorship. Repetition and dissemination of these words have historically been banned and deemed harmful to society. The ruling class made this determination, and these expressions, identified with those outside the norm, were cursed. Every community has a set of words that it accepts and even sanctifies. The source of the sanctity of the sanctified discourse is usually of religious origin. However, in bourgeois society, words such as "humanity," "society," "equality," "equality," "individual," and "freedom" have also been endowed with certain powers, and the community has begun to consider these words as sacred as prayers. Over time, the institutions formed established the "sacred," and each truth imposed its arguments on terms, and these transformed words were loaded with power. Every community that came together, every congregation formed or formed, equipped certain discourses with new powers and validated these discourses to the extent that they dominated the community.

Since the beginning of its evolution, human beings have never lived alone and independent of a community. The need for communication among living beings has increased with herding. The need to establish a relationship between the herd members develops in various forms and directions and gradually integrates with the environment and life of the living being (Teber, 2004, p. 152). As the herd becomes socialized and with the unequal distribution of surplus value, it has excluded and marginalized some people and made this marginalization effective through discourses. One of the main factors in this is the economy. Economic stratification has changed the balance of power. The discourse power of the economically prominent members of the community has increased. These discourses have become common discourses over time. The majority of the community melted into the paradigm of power and expanded the everyday discourse by producing propositions that circulated the common discourse and excluded the others. According to Lingis (1997, p. 119), any discourse between talking people is a struggle against outsiders, against those who spread interference and ambiguity, against those who have a vested interest in communication not taking place. Nevertheless, as communication occurs and some propositions are established as accurate, it labels outsiders as talking nonsense, as confused, insane, or violent, and often refers them to violence.

The power of words derives from their ability to define, and therefore to limit, beings and human relations. Words sometimes have class-specific qualities. Relations are formed between speech styles and the accumulation of capital. Spatial dispositives, which direct subjects and construct them, are structured and organized directly through language. They both enable social tendencies to produce human beings and serve as the carrier memory of these messages. According to Hacıkadiroğlu (2002, p. 25), if we call a human community that has come together only under the influence of social tendencies and has not yet encountered external forces that would disrupt this unity to a natural society, we can liken such a society to a living being. This organism is organized on the path of growth and development. The individual entities that make up an organism, such as cells, do what they can for its development and take their share of it. The sharing here is directly aimed at ensuring the development of the organism. It is inconceivable that any cell will receive a more significant share of nutrition than other cells because it is closer to food sources or because its function in the nutritional process appears more critical. Likewise, in a society that continues its natural development, it is conceivable that its organization and development conditions will determine the forms of participation and sharing.

We have looked at the evolution of the human being within the limits of the subject and at the historical development and change of the human being, which is the most obvious subject of the speech process. To some extent, it is necessary to describe society's evolution and examine its impact on speech. There are different ideas about the evolution of societies. Thinkers such as August Comte, Henry Morgan, and Karl Marx have pointed to a single line of evolution. Karl Marx's last work that can distinguish him from the other two is on the Asian Mode of Production and Ottoman Society. However, his life was not enough. Apart from single-line evolution, some thinkers advocate specific evolution and parallel evolution.

Single-line social evolution holds that all societies progress through the same stages immediately. Even if they fall back from time to time, every society will pass through the same stages, adapting to the necessities of cause and effect. Thinkers who oppose this view, which emphasizes the determinism of the economy, argue for original or parallel evolution. In original evolution, each community evolves according to its conditions. In parallel evolution, on the other hand, independent communities show the same essential characteristics when they are in similar natural conditions.

The central states, in other words, the states centralized by capital, evolve along the same lines. Some communities in anthropology are exceptions at this point. The development of civilizations is either single-line or parallel. However, especially after the Industrial Revolution, a single-line development has come to the fore, and the name of this line is capitalism. At every point it enters, it essentially uniformizes every culture as long as it is included in the production-consumption line, even though it allows diversity to the extent its final stage allows. Industrialization and post-industrialization cultures are becoming more and more uniform and, in the words of Guy Debord (2021), are turning into a *Society of Spectacle*.

The first pre-industrial societies were based on the family. However, the concept of "family" in these societies differs significantly from what we understand today. The family changes from society to society and from time to time. While conducting ethnographic studies, early anthropologists recognized the importance of the family concept for savage societies. The following statements by Conrad Phillip Kottak illustrate this:

> In Ivato, in the village of Betsileo, where I spent most of my time, a man named Rakoto was an excellent resource on the village's history. However, I asked him to work with me on the genealogy of 50–60 people buried in the village cemetery. He called his cousin Tuesdaysfather, who knew more about this. Tuesdaysfather survived the Spanish flu epidemic that devastated Madagascar and much of the world in the

1919s. Immune to the disease, Tuesdaysfather buried his dead relatives. So he knew about every person buried in the cemetery. Tuesdaysfather helped me with the cemetery genealogy. (Kottak, 2008, p. 32)

As you can see, Tuesdaysfather is used to genealogize the dead. Because in non-industrialized communities, family is a significant factor, and it is cultivated. Communities can be classified based on kin. Everyone is related to everyone else, and they spend most of their time with each other. In addition, living people, the dead, and the natural habitus are seen as family members. Conversations about life practices and the problems of the family or community are the leading conversational practices of everyday life. Collective prayers show the importance of speech and breath at that time and that prayers were made in crowds. Prayer practices include political events and rituals. The succession of words and actions stems from the belief in "Mana/Supreme Spirit." Mana is hidden in words and breath. According to these people, expressing actions with powerful breaths can influence future actions. These traditions that have come down to us are nothing but an activity that can be characterized as prayer. Prayer shows the importance of words and speech for societies.

In "savage" societies, there is no myth of the "individual," and these societies are classless. The person has yet to reach the point where they can feel like an individual and organize their life with this delusion. "Unbridled individualism is a modern product, not characteristic of primitive man" (Kropotkin, 2001, p. 88). It can be seen even in punishing a crime committed within the clan, the act of each individual binds the whole clan. Since almost nothing is done without a general vote, the community is responsible for the actions of its constituent subjects. Many acts are enacted after the tribal council has decided on them.

The following is well-known in the social sciences: some considered "savage" communities are equipped with mechanisms to prevent the emergence of coercive and oppressive power (Morgan, 1986; Levi-Strauss, 1997; Clastres, 2016). They have defense mechanisms against the emergence of unequal property relations. A mechanism similar to the state machine has evolved throughout civilization's history into a structure that is first tyrannical and then evolves into a structure aimed at survival. This type of power is not seen in these communities.

To briefly summarize the evolution of governance according to anthropological data, the lineage is egalitarian in terms of gender, and the main reason for this is that it is engaged in hunter-gatherers. Hunter-gathering brings this equality but limits the power and authority of the tribe's chief. Tribes switch to shepherding or hoe farming, and a status-based social stratification begins — the structure of status changes. There is status in every community, but the transformation of the economy makes status unnatural. These tribes are geographically limited. Power is still based on word of mouth, but recording systems have begun to appear. In the archaic state, agriculture was more developed, and class society was well established. There is a regional government based on kinship, and trust and word still dominate the actions of power. At the same time, however, weapons develop in parallel with the development of the class process.

So how did the state as we know it begin to take shape? Why did humankind create such a world? Jean Jaques Rousseau gave the philosophical answer to this question in the eighteenth century:

> The man who first encircled a piece of land with stakes said: This is mine, and found people gullible enough to believe he was the true founder of civilized society. Then someone came along, uprooted the stakes, and said to the people: 'Do not listen to this impostor! The fruits belong to everyone, and the land belongs to no one. If you forget this, you will perish!' he would have saved humanity from wars, murders, troubles, and disasters. (Rousseau, 1998, p. 59)

The diversity of the social division of labor that constitutes class societies and the conditions for controlling surplus value derived from agriculture have yet to emerge. According to Giddens (2021, p. 60), every human society requires a particular division of labor, albeit at a primitive level. However, the division of labor is at its lowest level in the simplest form of society, the tribe, where there is only a general division of labor between genders: women, whose job is essentially to raise children, play a less productive role than men. Men are initially purely communal beings; individualization is a historical product associated with an increasingly complex and specialized division of labor. There is an emotional hostility to private property, seen in the early stages of primitive communism. This hostility is related to the inability of the individual to see himself as independent of his community and nature.

As time progresses, a process of evolution towards this independence will begin in parallel with economic developments. Humanity still needs to have a consciousness that enables people to exploit people. How this consciousness is formed continues to be discussed in political philosophy and science. Concepts such as competition and property belonged to later periods when the state was formed. These concepts are still alien to savage societies. This alienation is linked to language, which is indisputable when we consider the reflections of every social phenomenon in language and its effects on language.

Humanity has been acquainted with power since the first periods of settled life. In contrast, when societies were still connected to hunter-gatherers during the transition to settled life, the institution of power differed from today. It is essential to examine the relations established between the people of hunter-gatherer societies and production to question the power of that period and to show that the power of that period was a power based on speech.

For the people of hunter-gatherer societies, production is an activity that is measured and limited by the needs that need to be met, i.e., the main thing here is the fulfillment of vital needs: Production is aimed at replacing the expended stock of energy. In other words, the living conditions, which must be considered synonymous with nature, create and determine the time necessary to reproduce this stock, including the amount society needs for festivities. In this case, once all vital needs have been met, nothing can induce these societies to produce more, that is, to waste time that could have been devoted to idleness, games, war, or festivities on aimless labor (Clastres, 2016, p. 152).

Community rules derived from tradition and experience prevent a class from forming in hunter-gatherer and tribal communities, where the community dominates the consumption of what is produced. However, humans producing for others and becoming alienated from their production would fundamentally change everything. A shift from pre-civilized society to civilized society was triggered by the development of mathematics based on the calculability of production activities - which was the goal of the first emergence of this science. The first seeds of the slave state were the first seeds of power based on coercion, which transformed society. These societies began to appear in history in the Neolithic Age. The Neolithic Age marked a transition from nomadism to sedentism, unlike the Paleolithic periods. Of course, this transition was not definitive and did not simultaneously carry all societies into a different era. The sedentary life in the Neolithic period led to population concentration and shaped the state apparatus. However, most sedentary societies initially maintained their economic structure based on hunting and gathering. Although they settled, agricultural practices dating back to 5,000 BC were not suddenly introduced in an advanced form. Thus, power in these societies was still based on the spoken word.

The fact that power is based on promises in establishing trust is present in power based on respect, not coercion or force, as in modern power. That is to say, the chiefs of clans and tribes have this power under their wisdom in battles or life practices. However, the community's approval is much more necessary than society's approval of contemporary power. The primary condition is that the community loves and respects the chief. Otherwise, the chief will be alone trying to resolve conflicts between the clan or community members with words and experiences. There is no law here. The chief resolves them verbally, such as talking about the ancestors who lived in peace, emphasizing that totemic beliefs support this issue, etc. The chief's success in resolving this issue depends on the strength of the community's respect, which does not necessarily mean it can be resolved.

No military class can legally enforce the chief's word, nor is there a religious caste that can validate that word among the people and put pressure on its implementation. The chief's power of oratory, the ability to use the word, is necessary for his prestige. However, the chief is not the holder of power, and the community members are the holders of power. The chief is certainly not and cannot be a despot. For the chief not to be, the community members and the community's traditions have power over this.

Usually, a chief would never think of trying to break the standard (proper) relationship with the community and move from being the servant of the tribe to being the master of the tribe. The great chief Alaykin, commander of an Abipon tribe in the Chaco region of Argentina, explains this relationship very well in his response to a Spanish officer who tried to persuade him to lead his tribe into a war he did not want: "The Abipons, by ancestral habit, do not act as their chief wants, but as they want to act. Yes, I am their ruler, but I will not do anything to their detriment. First of all, it would harm me. If I try to order or force my brothers and sisters, they will turn their backs on me. However, I want to win their love, not their hatred." Undoubtedly, many of the native chiefs would have said the same (Clastres, 2016, p. 159).

There can be no talk of rapid change in a social structure where power is based on promises. In such a structure, the chief cannot promise innovations to the people – and in any case, there is natural selection, not an electoral system based on promises. Innovation is not a good and positive concept for these societies. The subject of such a society does not live in search of novelty and difference. On the contrary, this human is in an evolution they cannot feel; it fears significant changes. It lives in a stabilized community with verbal assurance. Plans for the future have not yet become as complicated as they are today.

Two primary forms of democracy that existed in the development of early societies are discussed. The first is the compulsory natural democracy formed by people living in a hunter-gatherer-fisher basic economy, nomadic, and coming together only under the compulsion of natural conditions. There is no private property except for some personal belongings; the basis of life-economy is common property and the conditions of working together in solidarity. The word establishes more egalitarian relations between subjects. In these societies, there are no permanent and unchanging administrative apparatuses. Governance is more collective than today. It is collectively decided that skilled hunters and experienced people will lead and direct society for a while. However, this position is not hereditary. Moreover, the position of ruler does not bring any social and economic privileges to individuals. On the contrary, it requires excellent sacrifices from them (Teber, 2018, p. 155).

The development of production technology and the complexity of social relations brought about an evolution toward centralized governance. Certain families with more wealth had a more significant say in governance due to their concentration of social wealth. The riches were passed down as inheritances to the next generations. The opportunities provided by these riches led to the formation of classes and the widening of the class gap. In ancient societies, religious formations supported the retention of these riches, as did military forces. Toward the end of the last stage, the societies above evolved towards militant structures, which ended libertarian relations and ushered in slavery's first core features.

Religious preaching, one of the leading practices of power during the Middle Ages, is one of the practices of power based on the spoken word. The place of prayer is at the center of Christian churches. Since preaching was considered a religious duty, priests spoke in the streets, town squares, and churches. There are differences between the Sunday liturgy (sermons are dominical) and the festival liturgy (sermons are festive). In the eighteenth century, the 'masters of rhetoric' in the religious sphere were greatly admired (Briggs and Burke, 2021, p. 41). Another sphere of power in which oral communication was seen in the same period was the academies as the knowledge centers. Another type of oral communication is academic. In universities, students' logical ability was tested through conferences, formal discussions, and debates. Rhetoricians considered the art of speech (and behavior) as important as writing. In contrast, written texts, such as written examination papers, were not widely known in academic circles at the time. In grammar schools, the great emphasis was on Latin speech and the dialogues and games in which students practiced speaking (Briggs and Burke, 2021, p. 43).

In societies that have become more complex, the division of labor has increased, dominant-oppressed relations have grown, and writing has become a guarantee of power. It is impossible to find a sense of trust in communities based on the spoken word in class societies that have become more complex and populated. Urbanization and the formation of state bureaucracy increased the use of writing. In these societies, where theft and extortion increased due to the contradictions between the classes – these are the crimes created by the ruler-oppressed paradox – property relations and trade had to be based on writing.

However, since the seventeenth century, writing has been used by popes and kings for various practical purposes. Since then, writing has been used as assurance (Briggs and Burke, 2021, p. 18). Another factor that led to the development of writing was commercial activities. The recording procedures of merchants made writing necessary for society.

In this sense, the practice of power based on the spoken word was first based on the document with the invention of writing and then on recording after the discovery of sound and image recording tools in the twentieth century. The word is no longer a reliable instrument of human relations. The community has grown enormously, relationships and material practices have reached enormous proportions, and power based on the spoken word has weakened. It is no longer the word that guarantees the bureaucratic operationalization of a work or a becoming.

A different angle can be taken on the relationship between speech and power in addition to what has been explained so far. Bourdieu's philosophy, as is well known, divides the capital into four groups: material, symbolic, cultural, and social capital. Speech is the reflector of these capital groups. It is especially directly related to symbolic and cultural capital. In addition, another capital that can be added to these capital types can be defined as "sonic capital," a phenomenon related to biology and cultural value. Biological capital is defined as having positive qualities such as "beautiful," "touching," "pleasant," "sweet," "meaningful," etc., according to the aesthetic assumptions of the culture. According to the aesthetic assumptions of the culture, it is the possession of biological elements defined as having positive qualities. The tone of voice of the person delivering the speech is related to that person's biological capital. As well as being a source of meaning and content in speech, cultural capital is also a power source. In this sense, speaking is an indicator of capital and a channel of capital transfer. However, for this to be meaningful, it is necessary to be in the appropriate habitus, again within Bourdieu's conceptual framework (Bourdieu and Wacquant, 2014).

The speech reflects all forms of capital that affect habitus. It is related to the material, cultural, symbolic, and social capitals mentioned by Bourdieu, and since it is affected by all these forms of capital, it is their reflector. Furthermore, language is one of the most potent agents that directly establishes the structure of habitus. When two subjects start talking, they exchange symbols that reflect each other's habitus. The meanings and manner of speaking established by power and fed by various fields, various emphases influenced by psychology, and selectivity in perception are revealed in all the symbols of speech. Different forms of capital influence what is spoken about and what is not.

Speech, which has lost its value regarding the security and insurance of social relations and material world practices, is still a sign of power in personal communication and is a carrier of capital in various respects. The voice, the carrier of speech, is transformed into capital by taking on various value criteria of culture along with speech. This capital is the sonic capital.

Even though an image-centered, ocularcentric world has been established, sound is still the most significant meaning attachment and human speech is the most excellent carrier of meaning. The most evident proof is that the meaning conveyed by the silent image is much more limited than the meaning conveyed by sound without image (radio, podcasts, etc.). Sound without images can be followed, but the silent image is more difficult to follow. In this sense, the power of sonic capital is the most fundamental determinant of the image and is a direct apparatus of power.

Chapter 3

The Conversation is Locked Down

Language is the commonwealth of society. People develop their languages based on the cultural accumulation of the linguistic community in which they live, and these interactions make them subjects of society. The human is a being doomed to be a subject. In this sense, the notion of the "individual" is a nineteenth-century myth. There is no individual; there are subjects. The phenomenon of the "individual" with an independent emphasis is a myth. Because socialization makes people subjects, not individuals. The individual is in force as a legal and political concept, but the reality is that every human being is a subject.

According to Claude Levi-Strauss (1974), every culture has symbolic systems, including first language, marriage patterns, economic relations, art, science, and religion. While language becomes discourse in people's use, culture becomes discourse. Discourses are produced on a specific common ground in space, which is necessary for understanding. It may be nice for a speaker to present an academic text in a cocktail lounge accompanied by music, but this space will reduce the impact of the text. The speaker has to create the text depending on the social space. There are relations between the subject of the speech and the space. Social space produces the contexts of discourse and is essential for the target recipient of the discourse.

Social networks and management organizations have domesticated and influenced speech in many early societies. The processes of freedom and natural development of pre-property times were over. In the city-states of Mesopotamia, where enslaved people made up the bulk of the population, working conditions were so harsh that people did not have the opportunity to talk together. The relations of dominance between genders emphasized the male voice more than the other genders. When the city-state of "Ur" was dominant, work was imposed on large segments of society. The clergy began to manufacture consent to work, and the soldiers used coercion when necessary. Enslaved men were not allowed free time, while enslaved women were allowed one day off per month. However, many enslaved people died quickly under these conditions of hard labor and malnutrition. For example, according to one written document, 50 of the 175 enslaved people working in the temples died within a year; in another document, 14 enslaved people from a group of 44 enslaved people died within the first five months (Teber, 2018, p. 286). In these working conditions, people's ability to speak is limited. It is forbidden for enslaved people to talk to each other about anything other than their basic needs.

The ekklesia is another body established in the past that demonstrates the relationship between speech and power. "The form of government in ancient Greece favored public speech. Those counted as citizens could express their opinions openly and participate in policy and judicial decisions" (Jowett and O'Donnell, 2002, p. 27). The ekklesia were sub-assemblies in which every citizen in Athens – and even less than 10% of the male population were citizens – had a voice. Especially during the reign of Pericles, who consolidated his power in 446 BC, these institutions' voices reached a critical point. Opened to "who wants to speak?" these institutions operated at a time when the word was still the essential instrument of power. In reality, however, the most crucial function of the ekklesia in Athenian political life was ideological. By its very existence, it created and maintained a belief in the direct participation of the people in governance (Ağaoğulları, 2013, p. 45). As today's bourgeois parliaments, the ekklesia served not only as a screen in front of the high officials who ruled the country but also promoted the illusion of participation.

There are many periods of prohibition in the history of coffee culture. Early on, governments realized that coffee consumption increased communication and united people. They began to take measures and ban coffeehouses. In 1511, Hayr Bey, the governor of Mecca, feared that coffeehouses might become the centre of a secular revolt and ordered the closure of all coffeehouses. Anyone caught drinking or selling coffee was punished with beatings. The Cairo government, then in Mecca, reversed Hayr Bey's decision. However, the fear spread by the coffeehouses continued (Maspul, 2022).

Moreover, at these assemblies, only men were considered citizens. Enslaved people were excluded from politics. Speaking, especially politically, in a way that raises their voices now belongs to a particular class.

Throughout civilization, various examples of the lock on speech can be found in many geographies. The common point is to prevent enslaved people from realizing themselves and any resistance that may arise – preventing communication with each other aborts any uprising before it is even born. The prohibition of speech blurs the existence of the subjects and hinders their relationship with their selves, preventing the formation of class consciousness. It is only by communicating with the other that one produces one's self.

Six years before the outbreak of the Civil War, the astute New York observer Frederick Law Olmsted visited one of the first-class cotton plantations in the State of Mississippi and saw a large and beautiful mansion: 1,400 acres of land planted with cotton, grain, and other crops, and two hundred hogs. About half of the 135 enslaved people worked in the fields; three were artisans, and nine were hunting and stable servants. They worked from dawn to dusk every day except Sundays and sometimes Saturdays. In the Summer, those who worked in teams at the hoe worked continuously for 16 hours, with only a short break at noon to rest (Nevins and Commager, 2005, p. 194). A Black sergeant roamed among the enslaved people working in the fields and treated them as badly as the White men, encouraging them to work with whips. The plantation Olmsted describes is a much better plantation than the other examples. It is known that conditions were feral, and hundreds of people were killed on these plantations. Thousands of people were exploited under appalling conditions, whose families have been ruthlessly torn apart.

The word appears to be owned by no one at first glance. However, just like any other element of the Commonwealth, speech has also been subjected to appropriation by the government. Throughout the history of class societies, the spoken word has been censored, and communication between people has been limited. There was a ban on communicating with the emperor in the kingdoms of Far Asia. The emperor usually lived in a castle located at a great height, and it was impossible to reach him in a structure built with stairs, and it was forbidden to speak to him. Again, in the Middle Ages, the Inquisition forbade the use of certain words in society and severely punished those who used them. Most institutions attempt to take language under private ownership, which is a blow to the creative power of humanity. In today's postmodern world, the institutions still alive and left over from modernism – and the university is one – still judge the spoken word and its materialized form, writing, with formalism or scientific dogmatism because of evolutionary problems. All this hinders verbal expression, one of the most important of the ordinary riches of humanity, and strikes a blow to the everyday creativity of humanity.

The essential characteristic of the blow to co-creativity will be that not all people can participate in events and festivities. Today, most so-called "festivities" are passive events that people watch. Most mass events consist of catharsis-based spectatorship. In communal communities, however, all people are participants in egalitarian events. People no longer have an equal voice, and a minority group is producing the voice. We have moved away from storytelling's natural form and the qualities that make it unique.

The vast majority of ancient stories were the essence of phenomena that seemed supernatural because nature's physical qualities had not been discovered but were unified with human beings. This essence is called "mana" in anthropology. It is the essence of everything and the source of all action. The early communities saw all existence and themselves as parts and souls of "mana". Words are not the only tools that signify objects or phenomena and exclude concepts. They directly correspond to existence with its entire load of meaning. Therefore, the word would have a much more substantial impact on everything, especially the human body and mind, than it does today.

The vast majority of ancient stories were the essence of a whole at a time when the supernatural was unknown because nature had not been discovered to exist. The religious myths of antiquity and the fireside legends of ancient and modern times have their roots in the mental habits of primitive humanity. These myths and stories are the earliest records of people's sayings about visible phenomena in the world in which they were born (Fiske, 2009, p. 30).

The essential characteristic of the blow to co-creativity will be the prevention of the participation of all people in events and festivities. Today, most so-called "festivities" are passive events that people watch. Most mass events consist of catharsis-based spectatorship. The means of communication are the spectatorial apparatus of festivities. In communal communities, however, all people are participants in egalitarian events. The days when all people had an equal say were slowly passing away, and festivities became the production of a minority group. The vast majority of societies are equipped with various deprivations in disciplinary work.

The domestication of speech has been one of the main power functions throughout civilization. The domestication of speech is the domestication of humans. This is because the action is an event that can be organized through speech and interacts with speech. The primary condition for taking action is to speak and convey one's thoughts on action to another person. With modern domination, human beings have been prevented from openly communicating their inner world and expressing their thoughts on the outside world. One side of this obstacle is external pressure, i.e., censorship; the other is the obstacles created by the human constitution. The domestication of speech is nothing but the domestication of the mind and its harmonization with the system. Speech is not outside history, and since it is embedded in history, just like subjects, it is structured by all the elements of the system.

Throughout history, whoever has possessed the apparatus of power has also had the power to determine the content of concepts and, therefore, the content of speech. As an old Latin proverb says, "Caesar is also the master of grammar," "*Caesar dominus et supra grammaticam.*" To prevent human action, it is necessary to prevent the ability to think, and one of the oldest methods of power, which has been mastered since class societies came into existence, is censorship and silencing. Power implements this censorship and silencing in two ways. In times of crisis, it resorts to direct torture and oppression of subjects. However, direct repression and persecution undermine the functioning of the system. Since the beginning of its formation, the bourgeoisie has always defended freedom of movement and capitalist relations. It first fought against aristocratic culture and feudal relations to preserve this freedom. Then, it marched on its remnants by spreading its culture and dominating capitalist relations. To establish freedom of movement and trade in society, it destroyed all control mechanisms, including the planned economy. It attacked all kinds of social defense mechanisms such as religion, ritual, tradition, etc.

Until modern times, the dominant form of communication in the history of humanity was oral culture products. Knowledge was acquired in an ear-centered way through anonymous sources such as tales, rituals, and epics. In such a society where speech is dominant, the ability to rate is one of the essential skills a person should have, considering the conditions of the period. Using words correctly was one of the most critical assets of that period. However, this power lies in mesmerizing words. According to Le Bon (2009, p. 84), even when used skillfully, words and formulas eventually came to possess the truly mysterious power that magicians attributed to them. They could create terrible whirlwinds in the souls of crowds and soothe them. Only with the bones of those who fell victim to words and formulas could one build a structure higher than the ancient pyramid of Cheops. The power of words comes from the images they evoke in the mind, which are entirely different from their actual meaning. The words with the worst, most incompletely defined meanings sometimes have a significant influence.

By the thirteenth and fourteenth centuries, the bourgeoisie had become well-defined among the social classes, and by the fifteenth and sixteenth centuries, the Dutch, English, and French nobility were being bought. According to Sombart (1998, p. 19), especially in the two centuries between 1600 and 1800, a whole new social stratum emerged from the old nobility and the new monetary wealth, with a new wealth as its core and a primarily feudal way of life as its shell. Most rural peasants probably belonged to a mere listening public until the nineteenth century. In most cases, however, what they heard had been transformed into the print media of two centuries earlier. The storyteller was replaced by the literate peasant who read aloud what he chose from a plethora of cheap anonymous books and papers with folk songs written on them, distributed by peddlers. A very cheap 'popular' culture based on the mass production of outdated medieval vernacular novels had emerged long before the steam printing press and mass literacy movements of the nineteenth century.

Nevertheless, much of this production was consumed by a listening public, distinct from their contemporaries who read (Crowley and Heyer, 2017, p. 156). A reading public would be atomistic and would be constituted of introverted subjects. However, a listening public is a public more amenable to communication.

Europe's prosperity, especially from the seventeenth century onwards, was based on slave labor. Slave labor exemplifies precisely the points at which the conversation locks up. The criminal history of capitalism is based on the locking up of speech. The concentration of labor on work and the refusal to allow communication that might lead to rebellion are the hallmarks of the violent history of capital. The Portuguese and Spanish exploitation of Latin America from the sixteenth century onwards and the transport of silver mines to Europe, Britain's seizure of cotton plantations and textiles in India, the rubber seized by Belgium through torture in Africa and especially in the Congo, the industrial revolution and the coordination of companies that usurped the oil of the Middle East with Fordism, fulfilled the most critical need of industrialization called "importsubstitution." This is the capitalism that Walter Benjamin said: "Whatever you call civilization and wealth, blood flows underneath." Neo-liberal policies have transformed the violence and bloodshed seen throughout history into more symbolic violence and moved it away from living spaces and into prisons for war criminals behind closed doors or under the control of states. The twenty-first-century Guantanamo camp is just one of these examples.

Despite the soft propaganda of neoliberalism, one thing is clear. Opening the market opportunities of capitalism is built on violence and blood. Moreover, workers' speech was controlled while this building was being built. There are many examples of this. There will need to be more than the pages of this book to show them all. However, a few examples make it clear that the suppression of speech is a class condition. Valuable objects such as money, gold and diamonds are, in fact, the blood and sweat of workers historically.

During the early sixteenth century, the Spanish and Portuguese colonized the Azores and Canary Islands. They eradicated the resistant population. On the sugar cane plantations in the Canary Islands, it was forbidden to speak among the enslaved people. A hundred years later, in the mid-seventeenth century, the labour bottlenecks in the silver mines of Peru and Mexico were met by the Cacique (local chiefs) with forced labour from indigenous villages. In mines such as "Potosi," 4,000 meters above sea level, speaking is forbidden except for water and toilets (Biermann, Klönne, 2007).

When people are made to work hard and are prevented from communicating, it dehumanizes them. This prohibition of speech is perhaps why slavery lasted so long and did not end in a gigantic revolution, revolt, or uprising. Hyppolite (1997, p. 11) states, "when we cannot participate in discourse, we regress in humanity". Human life is always language-centred; without it, individuality is lost. Again, according to Deleuze (2020), meaning is essentially incorporeal. The incorporeality of meaning results from a commoning and meaning cannot be produced without commoning.

Not being able to communicate at work is a loss of meaning and maximum alienation. Being unable to speak is a collective rebellion and a blow to people's world of meaning. This must be a great torture that mechanizes human beings, which we twenty-first-century people cannot understand despite all the adverse working conditions.

In the Fordist era, when Taylor's principles dictated the organization of factories, speech was forbidden, but the worker at least had a body and a family and had the right to change places. However, as Foucault points out during work, the factory system, like other institutions of the society produced by Fordism, resembles prisons. Workers are expected to concentrate on work without talking. There is a profound gap between everyday life and the factory. As a practice of colonization that exploits the interior, Fordism regulates not only capitalist societies but also socialist states, which adhere to the same mode of production. Both how capitalism exploits bodies in factories and the forms of colonization imposed on countries internationally under the name of "bringing democracy" have continued in states that claim to be socialist.

Except for some examples of relatively independent socialism, such as Cuba and Yugoslavia, China and the Soviet Union, in particular, have deviated towards becoming colonial states. On the other hand, Cuba and Yugoslavia could not become colonies because of their position and conditions since every state colonizes when it finds favourable conditions and opportunities. Socialism colonizes life differently from capitalism. In the Soviet Union, a student had to get a job in whichever department graduated from university, and the state built the student's whole life. The city where they will live after their education is planned according to the needs of the state, and they are sent there. These people are never unemployed and have no future worries. However, they cannot make critical decisions about their lives; in a sense, their lives are colonized. If people refused to work for four months in a job offered by the state, they were guilty of "social parasitism" and could be sent to labor camps. Speech and communication were forbidden in factories, just like in capitalist states. In the Soviet Union, the socialist state attached great importance to social activities since consumer culture did not have narcotic qualities. Theatre, opera, and cinemas were accessible. However, there was severe censorship of the works of art that were screened. Narratives permitted by state ideology, such as the relationship between workers and bosses, the hostility of foreign countries against the Soviets, or the plight of the people in the pre-revolutionary monarchy, were free. Other topics require permission. Unsuitable subjects may be rejected, censored, and screened.

In the Soviet Union, with its overwhelming state hegemony, the subjects of speech and leisure time cultural activities were controlled and manipulated. Those that could not be controlled were punished. Free thought or party criticism is forbidden. The Soviet Union is undoubtedly the biggest censorship state in history. All states practice censorship, and every state marginalizes a group and manipulates or prevents its speech.

In the Soviet Union, with its overwhelming state hegemony, speech was manipulated and sometimes punished. Free thought or party criticism is forbidden. The Soviet Union was undoubtedly the biggest censorship state in history. All states practice censorship, and every state marginalizes a group and manipulates or prevents it from speaking. Nevertheless, the Soviet Union had the highest level of censorship. The Soviet Union was not an empire of evil as portrayed in Hollywood movies, but it was not a paradise as described by socialists. For example, it highly emphasized food protection techniques, and it was considered a state crime to introduce chemicals into the food the people ate.

Talking in factories that established assembly lines in the twentieth century was forbidden. The patient workers of the new industry work for eight hours, hardly ever leaving their seats and rarely even looking at each other. They are watched by Ford's snitches even when they eat in the fifteen-cent spaces they buy. Talking on the production lines is forbidden, and laughter is undesirable. Workers rarely speak and try to control their facial expressions. They rarely whisper to avoid the target of Ford's snitches. Ford's famous quote has gone down in history: "A factory is not a living room" (Biermann, Klönne, 2007, p. 113).

Henry Ford opposed workers' unions throughout his life and supported the mafia against workers' rights organizations in the United States. The prohibition of speech seen in the first examples of the production line is essential for the capitalist because of the mode of production and the new position of the workers. This way, the capitalist increases profits while initially aborting the workers' organization. The workers, whom they belittled and oppressed through symbolic violence with their status, preferences, and tastes, were also oppressed through the laws they produced through the mafia or lobbying.

The common characteristic of many socially accepted values also applies to status. In many respects, status stratification goes hand in hand with monopolizing spiritual and material values and opportunities. Alongside a certain status, which is always based on 'distance' and exclusion, there are all kinds of material monopolies and economic privileges. Privileges related to status include wearing unique clothes, eating particular foods that are taboo to others, carrying weapons, and having the right to engage in certain non-professional amateur artistic activities, such as playing specific instruments (Weber, 2008, p. 295). Considering the rigidity and permanence of status values, especially when the merchant classes were flourishing, it is evident that status indicators such as art activities, eating rituals and speech rules could not change suddenly. Therefore, the burgeoning bourgeoisie had somehow to possess the ranks and status-creating lifestyle of the past. For this, it started spending its money on the aristocracy's lifestyle.

In the seventeenth century, knighthoods were put up for sale, and a new status called "baron" emerged. Around the same time, the word "gentleman" became widespread in England. This word, derived from the word "gentry," denoted a kind of second-class nobility in England. Knights, who had high incomes because they held fiefs during the period of land ownership, were now being replaced by ranks such as baron and gentleman, which were not derived from blood but from property ownership. Squire and gentleman (of course, all of these have died out today – even in England – and are dying out as concepts) usually characterized independent men who lived off their rents or 'respectable' work. Before the mid-nineteenth century, it was widely accepted that one had to have a certain income level to be included in the Gentry (Sombart, 1998, p. 23).

The relationship between the income level and bureaucracy has strengthened throughout history, and the state has become a structure governed by income owners. Nation-states have inherited this relationship from the systems that preceded them. However, one of the most fundamental problems of the nation-state's relationship with speech is the effort to create unity based on a particular ethnicity. This is even more problematic in post-imperial nation-states such as France, Spain or Turkey. The languages spoken in the multi-ethnic structure of the empire were banned around the ideal of "one nation, one flag, one state." The natural and historical flow of speech has been interrupted for some people. The mother tongues of these people were locked down.

Under ordinary circumstances, people have passed down their languages orally from generation to generation for thousands of years. Languages have evolved, changed and entered into natural interactions with peoples' cultures. However, the nation-state has disrupted this flow and tried to spread the region's language, where capital is centred throughout the geography. It has continued to touch the language, sometimes directly and sometimes indirectly, through education and the media.

After adopting a unitary state structure, France, one of the European Union's founding countries, banned peoples' languages in the various geographies they dominated. In the ideology of "one language-one state-one nation," languages used by minorities have no place in official institutions. France imposed its language on its colonies through its official institutions. The most important reason for the marginalization and oppression of many minority languages in Western Europe is the ideology of the nation-state. The same State of France, when it has its language, devotes enormous resources to the propagation of this language. State support for disseminating a language can be explained by the expansion of the geography under the influence of that state. French language and culture courses are organized in approximately 130 countries worldwide to teach the mother tongue of French children and adults abroad. France has not taken protective measures for tens of ethnic languages such as Basque, Breton, Catalan, and Corsican within its national borders for many years. It has not allowed the right to mother tongue in education, citing the French Constitution. These groups, which are characterized as the historical minority of France, are the people who have lived in their lands throughout history. However, they have not been able to receive education in their mother tongue for two hundred years because French, the language of the people who founded the state, is not their mother tongue (Spolsky, 2004; Shepard, 2006; Wright, 2016).

Catalans and Basques are the best-known minority groups in Spain because they are famous for their struggle for language rights. When we analyze the situation in Spain historically, some very striking facts emerge. The Spanish Civil War of 1936–1939 was between nationalists led by General Franco and communists and anarchists. General Franco, who won the war, banned all languages except Spanish. He resorted to complete social engineering and attempted to exterminate the languages of the Catalans and Basques. Everyone living in Spain had to speak Spanish. People who spoke Catalan were tortured. No books, magazines or newspapers were allowed to be published in minority languages. Language bans continued until 1975 when Franco died (Payne, 2011; Boyd, 2020). After the 1983 normalization law, these bans were lifted entirely. Minority rights were granted after Spain joined the European Union.

The Republic of Turkey had a unifying definition of the people in the 1921 Constitution during the war, but after the war, with the 1924 Constitution, the first constitution after the establishment of the Republic in 1923, the state, like other nation-states, imposed bans on languages other than Turkish. The subjects of the state, consisting of Greeks, Armenians, Kurds, Arabs, Arabs, Laz and many other ethnicities, were called Turks. Assimilation policies were continued through resettlement policies, various pressures and the prohibition of mother tongue education.

Another crucial example of language bans in modern times is what happened during the Soviet era. The regime, which set out with the slogan of "comradeship-brotherhood," approached minority groups in a pluralistic and supportive manner during the Lenin era. Alphabets were developed even for small language groups. However, an incredibly repressive period began with Stalin, and a period of persecution, like capitalist states, began. In 1936–1937, it was made compulsory for everyone to use the Cyrillic alphabet. Education in Russian was made widespread. Stalin's persecution, especially of Turkic groups, has taken its place among the dark pages of history. Crimean Tatars were expelled from the places where they had lived for centuries, and their language and identity were tried to be destroyed. Similarly, Altais, Bashkirs, Kyrgyz, Kazakhs, Uzbeks and Yakuts could not receive education in their mother tongue (Gerovitch, 2004; Edgar, 2006; Dave, 2007).

For a long time, gender was also the hallmark of having status. Being a man added a higher status to all the facts you had, which was also reflected in the speech. Male speech, which carries the most prominent indicators of cultural capital, is a phenomenon that categorizes other genders and activates specific strategies on them. Gender and wealth are often seen as conditions for being able to speak. The fact that women and the LGBTIQA+ community remain in the background much more than men, and their discourse is suppressed, is as evident today as it has been throughout civilization. In a doctoral thesis conducted in Turkey in 2022, Gürel (2023) demonstrated the suppression of the discourse of the LGBTIQA+ community in mainstream newspapers, following the oppression of this community even today. According to Gürel, the only point where transgender people in Turkey can make their discourse heard is on the streets. They can only speak in the news about street protests. Other than that, they are represented and defined in the news by those who are ranked by society, such as doctors, police officers, and state officials.

Even though the post Fordist era, which emphasizes consumption, has led to a more egalitarian culture between the genders than in the past, male dominance persists today. This new culture, which emphasizes consumption regardless of its qualities and therefore strives to characterize a peaceful environment among all kinds of identities, has been causing significant changes since the 1970s to bring all people together in consumption and to create a new form of colonization by indexing everyone's lives to consumption.

After the 1970s, in the post Fordist periods brought about by new forms of production, the distinction between working and non-working time began to blur. Factories downsize and turn into enterprises. The mass labor force evolves towards skilled and qualified workers. Workers begin to receive continuous training through frequent meetings and workshops in offices and offices. Thanks to the worker leash called the cell phone, businesses cover all areas of life. Everywhere is now an office, and everything is for the development and training of workers.

Workers who were silenced by Fordism in the factories, in postfordism, speak in all areas, but they speak to improve their performance, and their whole time is now work-centered. They must constantly develop themselves in a work-centered way and constantly think about their work. In Andre Gorz's (2022, p. 25) terms, everything becomes commodified. Selling oneself spreads to all areas of life, and everything is measured in money. The logic of capital permeates all areas of life. There is no other way to sell oneself than to maximize one's skills. Workers volunteer to colonize all spheres of life, with no choice but to train themselves and become regulars in certification courses. In a space where all life is colonized, speech is entirely and utterly domesticated. It no longer needs to be banned. Andre Gorz sees this as transforming subjects' need to produce themselves into work (Gorz, 2022, p. 26).

Today, "the ability of the ruler (president, prime minister, or any other parliamentary idiocy) to differentiate oneself" through speech, as seen in the relation between speech and power, has weakened, especially in postmodern periods. In the late twentieth century, we observe that the people who run the state apparatus have succeeded in reaching out to the people by not using formal language like the rulers of previous eras. The Jacobin attitude toward modern power is being eroded day by day. The ruler with a style of speech closer to the people's everyday speech always has a much better chance in the next elections. The fact that the rulers are ordinary in their daily behavior and the words they use are close to the people's speech quickly covers their capital and class relations and influences the masses.

In a world where the immaterial dimension of products dominates their material reality (Rifkin, 2001), there is a parallel between the complete closure of people's discourse to their reality and the veiling of their inner reality by speech. There is no longer any lie. In an age where lies wholly surround truth, "truth" becomes only a matter of conformity to the self.

It has been a common characteristic of all forms of domination since the beginning of civilization for the masses to revolt against the symbolic dominance of capital. From the clergy to the military, from the despot to the aristocrat, many sovereigns have separated the working people and the marginalized segments outside the economy from themselves through their clothing, their everyday language, and many other lifestyle practices. They have put these life practices as a barrier between them and themselves. As a result of post Fordist production conditions enriched by the culture of imitation, these apparent practices have become somewhat similar to one another, blurring the divide between classes to some extent and giving the masses the illusion that their consumption habits are the same as those of the commodities they own, even if they are imitations. As a result of deprivation and poverty under the pressure of symbolic capital imposed by the rulers, this resentment has been engraved in the collective subconscious for thousands of years, giving rise to an urge to follow the evil capitalists, let alone explode as a social revolution. The natural desire of the herd of idiots who run after those who seem close to their life practices, at least in front of the cameras, is nothing other than the "will to power," as Friedrich Nietzsche put it. To be so easily caught up in the delusion that one is living the same life practices as the ruling character one identifies with and not to see the real class difference is the blindness created by the will to power, and the same will also detach people from actual class conditions.

Until we reach postmodern times, we see that those in power have separated their speech from the people as much as possible. The ruling minority invested its capital not only in weapons, police, and the military but also in art and knowledge. Words were as valuable as swords trying to maintain power in peacetime. From the era of city-states to the commercial states of Italy, from the Ottoman rulers with their divan culture to the Mandarin system in China, every ruling group sought to differentiate themselves from the people they exploited through language, another form of power based on speech.

Long before postmodern times, the bourgeois class, which tried to emulate the life practices of the aristocratic classes as much as possible to join them and emulate their way of life, created a new symbolic set by adding new ones to the way of life it had taken from the past to realize its "elitization" after dominating the world by taking over the political apparatus (by establishing republics and parliaments). Even in modern times, the petty bourgeoisie class imitated the lifestyle of the bourgeoisie. It is the fate of all lower classes to emulate the life of the upper class and to be tempted by the power of that class. They emulate those they see as powerful and the life produced by those they cannot have. The bourgeoisie, who create a hierarchy with all kinds of actions from how they speak to eating, from walking on the road to fashion, are separated from the people at every point, from art to consumer culture. Bourdieu (2021) summarizes that each class seeks to match the taste of the classes above it. In doing so, it also endeavours to separate itself from the lifestyle of the classes it sees as inferior.

This new class, which tries to make its life practices as similar as possible to those of the ruling classes of the period before the postmodern times, emulating their way of life, has created a new symbolic set by adding new ones to the practice of energy it has taken from the past to realize its utilization after dominating the world by taking over the political apparatus (by establishing republics and parliaments). They created a hierarchy with the care given to all kinds of actions, from how they spoke to eating, from walking on the road to fashion; they were separated from the people at every point, from art to consumer culture. Women were seen as ornaments everywhere modernization began. They made ornaments by caring for their clothing and education, proving how much we discussed has dominated their lives. Thorstein Veblen, in his work describing the nineteenth-century world, expressed this situation as follows:

> At the stage of economic development when women are still strictly the property of men, ostensible idleness and consumption performance have become part of their desired services. Since they are not their masters, the visible spending and idleness of women increase the credit of their masters rather than themselves. Therefore, the more expensive and unproductive the woman of the house is, the more admirable and effective her life is for the reputational purposes of the household and its head. (Veblen, 2005, p. 123).

In his work "Theory of the Idle Class", Veblen explains how the bourgeois class separates itself from the working class with all its actions. This process affects, of course, a fundamental communication activity, such as speech. The distinction between the people's language and the palace's language has been indispensable for class oligarchies since immemorial times.

In postmodern times, external pressures are breaking down daily. However, the forces on language live on in all kinds of relations, objects, and subjects through dispositive. At this point, defining a dispositive to clarify the issue would be helpful. Michel Foucault used the concept of dispositive to refer to the material and intellectual mechanisms that produce subjectivity. According to Negri and Hardt, the dispositive is a formation whose primary function is to respond to a demand at a given historical moment. The dispositive is thus a specific manipulation of the power relation of power. It has an enormous strategic function, which means it involves a rational and regulated intervention with those in power relations to either develop them in a specific direction, hinder them, make them more stable, or benefit from them. The dispositive is, therefore, always defined by a relation of power. It is permanently bound to one or more limits of the knowledge from which it originates and simultaneously conditions it (Hardt and Negri, 2011b, p. 136). The production of the subject through dispositive is a never-ending process and continues throughout life. Thus, speech, the most crucial element reflecting the issue, is also shaped within this production. It is suppressed or developed and supported at specific points. However, this is not an act but a passive function.

In Pierre Bourdieu's philosophy, language is the means of transmission of cultural capital. As money is the symbol of economic capital, language is the fundamental symbol of cultural capital. Aspects such as the form of speech, its relationship to the central dialect, the approval of its meaning by legitimate aesthetes or scientists, etc., contribute to understanding the ownership relations of cultural capital embodied in speech. Just as class distinctions take shape in tastes and preferences, internalized words take a position in the available spaces conveyed in speech and in the central or outlying dialects through which speech is transmitted. The question "Does the content of speech consist of common discourses shared by ordinary people, or is it concentrated in a more singular location?" involves an answer related to the concentration of cultural capital.

People speak by producing common discourses in the delusion of individuality, and the uniqueness in speaking is dulled. The community always establishes this commonality, but at the point we have reached today, this commonality is established artificially. National identities, religious communities, etc., are all the products of a certain artificiality. Zygmunt Bauman describes how, in a census conducted in Polish villages in the late 1930s, the villagers could not understand the phenomenon of "attachment to a nation." The villagers gave answers such as "We are from here," "We belong to this village," and "Our grandfathers were from this village" and failed to understand the questions of the officials (Bauman, 2022, p. 27). Forming an identity because one has a nationality is not a natural phenomenon. Concepts such as "homeland," "nation," "flag," "man," "woman," "names of people," etc., which are the foci of insurance and assurance of the system, are foci of ordinary discourse and meaning that prevent ambiguity and blurring. These are the anchoring nails that try to prevent fluidity and uncertainty.

Who is speaking today? Do people make judgments in their own words? What is the concept of "we" seen in many discourses? Who is the "we" that stands out in discourses, reduces multiplicities to unity, and homogenizes them?

At the end of the nineteenth century, there was a period in the Americas and Europe when those with nothing but their labor could unite, join unions, and engage in struggle. Ethnically inhomogeneous and ethnically diverse communities settled in harsh working conditions among the factory machines and participated in strikes, protests and speeches in political organizations through collective movements. The expectations of the poor and economically precarious were much lower than those of today's middle classes, and they were able to form a unity that could fulfil these expectations. Most did not expect their children to attend university or move up in class. With these facts, they could meet in a real "we." The nineteenth-century workers' movements had a unique strength because they had yet to move away from these real collectives. The "we" dominated over the "I."

However, over time, factors such as nationalism and state support for various religious sects, the growth and development of the petty-bourgeois class thanks to the diversity of consumption in the public sphere, the concentration of capital created by the exploitation of other continents in the Americas and Europe, the domestication and taming of the working class, the increase in individualism thanks to radio and later communication tools, the spread of full employment and mass consumption silenced people in geographies where capital was concentrated and integrated the opposition into the system. Welfare and these privatizations disintegrated the collectivity of the working class in particular. The industrialization and mass consumption of clothing and cosmetics from the 1960s onwards, and the speed of post Fordist production from the 1970s onwards, increased subjectivities. This was carried to its peak with the neo-liberal policies of 1980. Television, which entered living rooms and even bedrooms, increased individualization and subjectivities in physical spaces but also brought a new "we" and a delusion of collectivity in consciousness.

The rise of the service sector in offices, clerkships and bureaus in the twentieth century, the fact that the female labour force could take part in the production sectors as much as men, and especially the shrinking of factories and the emergence of different office systems due to the post Fordist production qualities; increased the phenomenon of "us" constructed in minds instead of a real collectivity. Every lifestyle, every ethnicity, every gender and, more interestingly, every way of eating constituted little "us." These small "we"s, formed as an oppositional political movement in 1968 and were anti-capitalist, were now integrated into the system and turned into communities that produced fashion and niche areas of consumption diversity in various sectors.

With postfordism, new "us"s could be produced, supported and incorporated into the economy as niches.

Pierre Bourdieu begins a speech describing the positioning of men and women in a community he studied in Kabul with the question, "Who is speaking?" This question is vital in describing the locking up and domestication of speech. Bourdieu replies, "It is 'we' who speak." Moreover, he explains that educational institutions create the phenomenon of "us" by creating a collective consciousness. According to Bourdieu, the subject in most behaviours, thoughts, and contemplations is not a personal "I" but a transpersonal "we". People who go through similar family patterns and almost identical educational curricula learn about the "we" phenomenon, build it in their minds and build their predispositions on it. The system brings individuals together in a "common world of meaning."

Bourdieu's "common meanings" and what I call "common discourses" and "blocks of meaning," the system's fuse foci of intense energy such as "homeland," "nation," "flag," "God," etc., which are familiar due to frequent repetition and are not questioned almost as if they are innate, create a collective consciousness by using all mouths thanks to the "we" consciousness that transforms each person into an agent of the system.

Today's communicative cultural agency and speech are circulated and cultivated in the predispositions of subjects' preferences and discourses that no one mainly does but which culture reproduces by subjectivizing each individual. These fuses are articulated in various tendencies and predispositions. Tendencies and predispositions are the will to power produced by the accumulation of anger due to deprivations in various areas of capitalist life, the wounds inflicted on subjects by forms of symbolic violence, the inability to reveal the emotions on which mental energies depend or their blocking by being locked in the minds, people who cannot develop and reveal their true potential due to alienated production; the obtusions (A state of numbness and insensitivity in medical literature) experienced due to passive watching of the festivities. Tendencies and predispositions stand ready to marginalize in various ways "foreign" discourses outside of the insurance foci on which common discourses depend.

The "we," the system itself, speaks through each individual's mouth. The system, which locks up speech and turns all mouths into one, can function thanks to subjects that can be manipulated without external pressure. Henceforth speaking is a docile, domesticated, and constantly fed act.

They had deceived grandmothers and grandfathers; they deceived their parents; they are deceiving the people of today with powerful means of discourse, and the children who play today will be deceived tomorrow with more powerful weapons. It is time to stop all this and silence the government that speaks through the mouths of the people because people who have been turned into parasites have reached the power to destroy the ecology in partnership with those who have nothing in common.

A kind of discourse and opinion-generating military force, they engrave discourses into people's minds. These can be called symbolic military forces. They are embedded in the ideological apparatus and as if in unison, uphold the shields of discourse that constitute the protection of power. Supporters of neo-liberal policies, a considerable number of academics, media-loving agitators with various titles and ranks, psychologists, sociologists, and social workers, a growing number of new age gurus, new astrologers, and many others produce discourse by leaning on the capitals organized by the government. They are the symbolic military force of the system, which has lumbered the minds of its followers.

To summarize the domestication of speech in one sentence, we can say the following: The domestication of speech is speaking without saying anything. The power that speaks through the mouth of each individual says nothing. To speak without saying anything, minds must become clumsy. They sow their polished discourse in society by constantly having their media butlers, organic intellectuals, and media-friendly intellectuals say what they want. They say nothing to produce the same mind. The contexts give a sense of renewal due to the change of subject, space, and subjects. However, since they say nothing and play with extras, opinions always remain the same and cannot add renewal to life. The intellectual clumsiness of ordinary people liberates power behind the figure of the strong leader. A strong leader is a sign of a weak society with clumsy thinking. When mental clumsiness becomes mass, human beings are one-dimensionalized, and a mental structure capable of rebellion is destroyed, there is no need for the state and prisons.

Chapter 4

Prison Becomes Wallness

The tradition of beginning the history of humanity with writing is one of the impositions of the progressive perception of history. After the end of the last ice age, usually, nature no longer threatens often human life. The world, which has yet to enter a severe global climate crisis, is structured with knowledge produced from a foundation centred on human beings and civilization. A stable climate has built in us the delusion that we are at the center of existence. Human beings are a species that will not be able to understand reality until there is a break in this climatic stability. The reality is this: the human is not at the center. Spectators and a few actors look at the stage and think it is fixed. When they realize that the whole hall, including the stage, is not a fixed and infinite structure, they will see that many problems in everyday or political life are magnified. The costumes and décor have changed over time, and the number of spectators has increased, but the stage has remained unbroken and stable for a while. While the actors are accessible on the stage, on the other side of the theatre, where the majority is, they have built prisons in various ways. They have separated the "good" from the "bad" and created walls. Since they cannot see that the Anthropocene era is about to destroy the hall, they have an unconditional belief that these prisons will remain in place.

The progressive understanding of history taught in many schools tells us that human beings are at the center and are the only creatures of the universe. However, the "green history" presented by authors such as Clive Ponting (2012) emphasizes that this is not the case. Will it be too late when history, which is drawn as progress, realizes that this progress is destruction?

The understanding of history read as progress produces the illusion that speech has also been liberated. Were the "welfare states" established after the Second World War democratic? Is speech now free, contrary to many examples in the history of civilization? Does not the fact that prisons are no longer a place of confinement for many crimes give some clues? Why are these crimes no longer damaging the system? Why has speech been freed more than in the past?

The latest attack on humanity by the bourgeoisie, which has replaced common sense and control mechanisms in society with the capitalist understanding of freedom, especially after 1980, is to imprison subjects in the perception that they are disconnected from each other. There are parallels between the development of neo-liberal policies and the increase in crime rates. People live in fear more than in the past and feel total insecurity. For consumption to be increased, collectivity must be reduced. Wherever consumer culture is spreading, walls are breaking down. Rules are bent and changed so that everyone becomes a consumer. Censorship is eliminated, and speech is encouraged in every medium. Information content is not essential; it is the consumption of information that matters. As Chul Han points out, it has become clear that more information only sometimes leads to better decisions. Society can tolerate a vacuum, neither in information nor in vision. However, thought and inspiration need space (Chul-Han, 2022a, p. 19).

In such a society, there is no longer any need for censorship by the government. There is no thought of being censored anymore, which makes the highest stage of the production society uncensored and "democratic." Resolving conflicts and problems that could lead to conflict in favour of the power and against the oppressed and accepting this solution by the people has calmed the environment. Rereal violence in all its forms has been removed from living spaces, and rules have been put in place for the smooth functioning of capitalism. There is no longer any idea that can produce opposition. Those that exist have been domesticated.

In periods when thought could not be controlled by symbolic military power and when different ideas could meet the masses and exist, the need for censorship by the government is related to its ability to protect the structure. It was once possible for an idea to spread to mobilize the masses. It could influence and change the social order to the detriment of the rulers. Censorship is an archaic act from these times. There is no need for censorship in geography with an abundance of capital.

On the contrary, different ideas are supported because they can open up new niches, and everything can be wrapped in the warm arms of economics. Because this society is the information society that developed after postfordism, this is a period when the most severe issues can be tabloidized, when rap music can be an effect behind a rap song in the frivolous social media channels. There is no seriousness because the maximum viewing time is three or five seconds. There needs to be more time to take a subject seriously. If some take it seriously, they can do so because of the comfortable lifestyle offered to them, which is their job. There is no censorship because the content of information has been emptied, and the power of the complete information has been broken. Speech is now domesticated, and the walls of the prison are blurred. The whole society is a giant prison that resembles an amusement park, a fairground.

The ideas that have dominated societies throughout history have never been so integrated into the ruling classes. The essential quality distinguishing human beings from other living beings is the ability to analyze symbols. The subjet's mental activities, which produce ideas within the structure, are derived from matter. Within the limits of the material world, he has many ideas. Despite this, the minority maintains its power by injecting ideas into subjects supported by the state apparatus. Thus, it owns property and surplus value unequally because the system functions. Karl Marx summarizes this situation in his work "The German Ideology" as follows:

> The thoughts of the ruling class are, in all ages, the ideas that dominate society; in other words, the type that is the ruling material force of society is also the ruling mental force. The class that holds the material means of production also has the mental means of production. They are so intertwined that the thoughts of those not given the standards of mental output depend on this ruling class. Sovereign ideas are nothing but the intellectual expression of sovereign material relations. Sovereign ideas are material, sovereign links conceived in the form of ideas. These ideas, then, express the concerns that make a class the ruling class. (Marx and Engels, 2004a, p. 75).

Until half a century ago, the state was the most crucial producer of knowledge in almost every nation-state. Today, this is no longer the case, even in underdeveloped countries. The Internet and corporate media produce far more information than the state. Children learn much more from social media than they do at school. However, in totalitarian countries, the state continues to censor because, in the geographies dominated by these states, there is either no abundance of capital or, if there is, it is protected by the very structure that this censorship needs.

In an area where the activities of the state expand, the area of dissemination of state-produced information also expands. The state controls the flow of information in society according to the ruling class's interests. In the course of this control, it censors information that it does not deem in line with its interests, which may create interference in the flow that provides its rent. Information that goes beyond the dominant information disseminated by the system and the frequency of any medium disseminates this information is silenced. This silencing can be through direct coercion or economic marginalization methods, as happens in totalitarian and authoritarian states. In Turkey today, the Recep Tayyip Erdoğan regime silences an opposition TV channel or imposes very high monetary fines almost every month, one of the ways the Erdoğan regime survives. Because through such repression, capital maintains its flow rate since it has no opposition. Turkey's decline from 2002 until today is precise because of this attempt to push life along with a reduced intensity of democracy.

Ideas outside the dominant information are excluded from mass broadcasting because media-related institutions require capital. Dissenters allowed by the dominant information are censored during periods of heightened conflict. Moreover, since the number of these dissidents is small, they need help finding a place in the capitalist information flow based on advertising, ratings or readership. Their discourse becomes marginalized. They are excluded from areas dominated by the market economy. Being able to produce information is related to material capital, and the passive exclusion from the economy of those who do not produce what the masses want is another form of passive censorship.

Populism, the tendency to produce the wishes of the masses, dominates society with sovereign information consisting of a bundle of messages that keep the herd entertained, numbed and distanced from the realities of society, avoiding information and preserving the static. It reduces the entertainment phenomenon to screens and transforms people's understanding of participatory entertainment through genuine relationships into watching/viewership. Outside the show, the oppositional bundle of information is marginalized and cannot find representation. Every idea is considered legitimate as long as it participates in the show. The ability to dissent ideas to reach large masses will prevent the principles that determine the system's functioning from gaining legitimacy and, thus, will deal a severe blow to the system's production of consent. The delusion that events are natural is necessary and even indispensable for subjects. However, some subjects, even if they remain in the minority day by day, can escape the waves of dominant information to some extent. According to Han (2022, p. 23), over-information and over-communication are symptoms of a lack of truth and a lack of being. More information and more communication do not eliminate the fundamental uncertainty of the whole. It increases it even more.

Power achieves an effective self-direction over the lives of the entire population only through the mass cultivation of consciousness or the capture of each individual from the universal anthropological roots of emotion, such as fear, famine, etc., which provide their psychological motivation. It is a flow that passes from person to person and is reshaped in each person, like total energy that encompasses life. As Foucault says, "Life has now become the object of power." The most important function of power is to encompass life in all its aspects, and its primary task is to rule life. Biopower, then, describes a situation in which the main issue for those who master its tools is the production and reproduction of life itself (Hardt and Negri, 2003, p. 48).

The fact that speech is a prison is also noticeable when one looks carefully at the phenomenon of time in "synonyms." Time grasps speech in different ways. There are no words that are synonyms of each other because they were born at different times and are the product of different contexts. There are no synonyms. No word can be equal to another. It can be close, very close, but not equal. There is equality in different languages, but two words in the same language cannot equal each other, specifically when the time factor comes into play. One of the words has a different layering of meaning than the one used in previous times. Time encompasses and assimilates the word. From another point of view, the times that Tense points differ from culture to culture. Because just like every culture, every language has a different perception of time. Some societies do not have a future tense in their language.

Time is the most powerful phenomenon that affects all phenomena that human consciousness comprehends. Humans cannot comprehend it because it is so evident in their daily lives. No known and sensed being can be thought and comprehended independently of time. Evans-Pritchard, who studied the Nuer in Sudan in the 1930s, realized that this community had no more than a two-year future (Evans-Pritchard, 1986). The perception of time is not independent of the other elements of the structure of human consciousness.

In today's working process, time is controlled rather than "earned," it is no longer the Fordist factory bell or the boss who controls it. Subjects themselves are directly made the boss of their entire existence. They appear more accessible in their choices than ever before. They are programmed and locked into success and what they will do by an internal mechanism. Time is difficult for the system to control. As a result, the exploited subject's cooperation was needed to achieve this. The best way is to make subjects control themselves. The control must become self-control (L'Heuillet, 2022, p. 22-23).

Another imprisoning element of speech is seen in gender inequality. Speech is male. All over the world, men speak. It infects all genders. Who dominates the structure, dominates the language and is the master of speech. If dominating is considered a weakness, everything "male" can be considered weak. It is rigid, too rigid to grasp life and vitality. Because it is a sign of alienation and detachment from the self, in this sense, it is the person who is lacking. That is why it demands power and speaks through power. All existence flows into the void called "man", which is such a big void still to be controlled. Language responds to the gravitational force of the idea of "man" black hole and is drawn towards it. The speech of the other genders also becomes masculinized or is influenced by it.

Jacques Lacan is one of the thinkers who has carried the determinism of language to the highest point. Jacques Lacan, one of the post-structuralist thinkers, does not accept the structuring used by Saussure for language. He disregards the effect of grammatical structure on speech and rejects all distinctions between the subject and society in the context of language. According to Sarup, Lacan emphasizes that people become social by adopting language; the language makes them subjects. Therefore, according to Lacan, the individual and society should not be seen as separate. Organisation inevitably carries each individual within themselves. Lacan's view is this: Biology is always interpreted by the human subject and refracted and reflected by language; therefore, there is no such thing as a 'body' before speech. Lacan thus shifted all descriptions from a biological-anatomical level to a symbolic level, showing how culture can impose various meanings on anatomical parts (Sarup, 1997, p. 21). According to him, knowledge of the self is acquired through language. The way for the subject to recognize itself is through language. In other words, there can be no subject independent of language.

Lacan's statements support the claim that speech is male. According to Luce Irigaray (2006, p. 32), masculinity attributes the ownership of goods to itself. It gives its gender type to God, the sun, and the laws of the universe. Moreover, it does this behind the appearance of "neutrality." By ignoring the discursive dimension of culture, allegedly neutral technology and various colonialisms remain dominant. Whether directly or indirectly, the "man" wants to give his gender to the universe.

Luce Irigaray, just like Lacan, rejects the distinction between society and language. According to her, language is formed by the linguistic sediments of previous ages. Language reflects the modes of social communication of the time. Each age creates its ideals and imposes them on subjects as ideals. Step by step, these ideals leak their norms into discourse. The gender hierarchy determines the language and is determined by language. Gender identities other than males have no chance to speak culturally and assert their speech. Women are forced to speak like men to take a position (Irigaray, 2006).

With the ability to say "no," which is one of the foundations of human existence and perhaps the only inherent characteristic of human nature, humans sometimes generate ideas against the dominant thoughts. At this point, they go outside the paradigm of the system. The sovereigns who dominate biopower cannot control all life. Life is too infinite to be held. As Deleuze puts it, life becomes a resistance against power when power targets energy. "They will not win unless they find a way to destroy the human imagination" (Zamyatin, 2019, p. 232). Breaking out of the dominant paradigm of the system, especially in times of crisis in underdeveloped countries, requires intervention in ideas that can turn into action and even guide the movements of the masses. When the state apparatus cannot produce consent, it resorts to force. Censorship is one of these instruments of coercion, perhaps the oldest.

After the various locks on speech created by the dualities of language and time, language and gender, let's turn to an external lock: censorship. Censorship is one of the oldest punishments in the history of civilization. With the invention of writing, especially in the late Middle Ages, censorship emerged as a phenomenon with a vast network of users by the state apparatus. An institutionalized state is necessary for its systematic implementation. Anaxagoras' punishment, who lived in the fifth century BCE in Ancient Greece, was exiled for saying that the sun was a pile of stones considered to be a god; Socrates for allegedly corrupting young people by talking to them and for his speeches to the people who tried him in court; and the torture death of Dervish Mansur al-Hallaj by the rulers of the Islamic regime in the tenth century because his words threatened state security are examples of censorship in the process of oral culture. They would not have been silenced if Socrates or Hallaci Mansur had not been killed.

The historical perspective of the domestication of speech results from an evolution from a disciplinary society to a surveillance society. In a society where speech is the antithesis of power, where the mass of workers in old-style production is concentrated in factories, laborers cannot afford to move much spatially. They are seen as production mechanisms crammed into a factory and can be moved at most a few times in their lives. Punitive practices and exclusion are sufficient to silence and intimidate them. However, thanks to the expansion of communication devices, the possibilities for people to communicate with each other have increased. This time, however, it is seen that the whole set of dispositive called "life" domesticates human beings and, therefore, domesticates speech. A human being born into a world of discourse is too enmeshed to realize its artificiality. It has become too small in the system to realize that all the signs around it are agents of the system. This shrinking is proportional to the growth of the society people live in. The surveillance society has established a much more successful power than the disciplinary society thanks to the power it has implanted in the brains and has destroyed the potential of people to rise against the power, their ability to be together, and thus their mass movements.

The historical perspective of the domestication of speech results from an evolution from a disciplinary society to a surveillance society. In a community where speech is the antithesis of power, where the mass of workers in old-style production is concentrated in factories, laborers cannot afford to move much spatially. They are seen as production mechanisms crammed into a factory and can be forced a few times in their lives at most. Punitive practices and exclusion are sufficient to silence and intimidate them. However, thanks to the expansion of communication devices, the possibilities for people to communicate with each other have increased. This time, however, it is seen that the whole set of dispositive called "life" domesticates human beings and, therefore, domesticates speech. As a result of being born into a world of discourse, human beings cannot see its artificiality. The system has become too small to realize that all the signs around him are agents. Its shrinking is proportional to the growth of the society in which it lives. The surveillance society has established a much stronger power than the disciplinary society but has also destroyed people's ability to unite against the regime and, therefore, their mass movements.

Disciplinarians fixed individuals within institutions but failed to enclose them entirely within the practices of production and the rhythms of productive socialization; disciplinary society has not fully penetrated the consciousness and bodies of individuals of addressing and organizing individuals in the totality of their actions. In a disciplinary community, the relationship between the individual and power is static: the penal expansion of power is met with resistance from the individual. On the other hand, when power becomes biopower entirely, the entire social structure is designed by the control mechanism and develops within its framework. Society reacts as a single body under an influence that reaches down to the nerve endings of social structure and development processes. Power thus manifests itself as a control mechanism that penetrates deep into people's consciousness and bodies and all social relations (Hardt and Negri, 2003, p. 49).

There is a parallel between the domestication of speech and the transformation of the form of punishment for thought crime. The development of these two superstructural phenomena is linked to capitalist relations, which are fundamental to transforming the concept of power. Punishment practices in the West evolved into a different dimension from the modern period. In societies where capitalism did not exist, it is seen that the body has no value and the treatment of it in all kinds of punishments results in violence. In these societies, power is coded to inflict pain and harm on the body, to destroy or destroy it because the body is not yet at the point of being an object of consumption and the basic unit of the system. As capitalism evolved into a system in which every part of the subject is exploited, it had to develop the apparatus of biopower. The body is no longer an object to be destroyed; it has to be glorified and disciplined, and every part of it has to be recorded with photographs and digital expressions. As Michel Foucault puts it, modern power is the great detention.

People in great detention live with a subconscious fear of capitalist life practices. The large masses who are hopeless about the future and therefore anxious take on the typical reaction of people who experience anxiety. Fear is one of our primary emotional states that rescue people from their situation and provide them with the necessary energy to create a refuge. Human reactions are accelerated by biochemical processes that automatize behavior in case of fear. "The more compelling the threat, the greater the likelihood of incoherent and unnecessary gesture, or, conversely, of inertia that risks not being pragmatic. This irregularity of movements is often accompanied by a decrease in intellectual abilities and attention to reality" (Mannoni, 2009, p. 10). The narrowing of the mind and actions is proportional to the individual's mind sensing danger. Ideas are fuzzy, and movements are disorganized.

In addition to the fears generated by terrorism, wars, climate disasters, earthquakes and so on, which are periodically felt in many parts of the world, some anxieties have been imposed on every aspect of life. Precariats, flexible production workers who cannot foresee what tomorrow will bring, a large mass of precarious and uninsured workers, and the anxious life course produced by neoliberal policies distract many people from intellectual and artistic activities. The hopes and welfare state projects that never materialize for most of the world make Horkheimer's "mental eclipse" of Hitler's Germany valid for the whole world. This version of capitalism generates constant fear and anxiety for the masses and does not create a sustainable life.

Large masses cannot collaborate during fear. Humans are accustomed to living in groups of 100–150 people in nature, so they have yet to evolve to act in masses. A group of fish, millions of fish, do not experience confluence. However, humans are open to the danger of stampedes in a crowd because they have not encountered such mass movements in the evolutionary process. Therefore, crowds need to be figured out. Such a crowded city life, giant metropolises, necessitates a capacity far above the community consciousness humans have developed in the evolutionary process. People of postmodern society lack the evolutionary powers to adapt to city life. The city kills the human. It pushes it to a life of extreme isolation as if reacting to an excessive transmission. Life is a set of actions that have become a defense mechanism against these vast crowds. Speech practices that are so shallow and robotized are like a social hysteria caused by unaccustomed massiveness.

Crime and punishment vary according to time, the geographical location of the masses, modes of production, and societies' power structures. Both crime and punishment are determined by culture. With the formation of class societies and the development of the apparatus of power, political crime began to be mentioned, which can be traced back to the beginning of the state apparatus. In all class societies, the ruling classes impose their ideological structures and the dominant paradigm on society through various means of producing consent, often by force. This process is a sine qua non-condition for preserving social order and the necessity of the rule of these classes. The phenomenon of political crime and punishments for it vary from one society to another, but it is found in every society where power apparatuses are formed.

So how is it that speech, once a criminal act, is now more accessible in many societies than in the past?

The eighteenth century is a period in which the seeds of the formation of today's penal system can be seen, and some changes in the West make this clear. In the medieval system of punishment, which operated with various strategies that could inflict pain on almost every part of the body, we can see a period in which power completely dominated the subject. The power symbolized in the king or the sultan, in other words, the despot, now wholly dominated the subject. In the past, unlike today's ownership, power could not address desires. Since it does not have the necessary technologies to address desires, it produces fear, or power itself reproduces and multiplies in the same common discourses with society.

However, with the transformation of the body into an economic value with modernity and its great gaining value for the system in consumption rather than production, a significant transformation in punishment practices is noticeable. Punishment is no longer based on inflicting pain on the whole body but on momentary contact with it and a secret contact away from the eyes of the other subjects that make up the community. The reactions to the announcement of the crime and the ostentatious theatrical presentation of punishment have increased with the rise of human rights. Although punishments and tortures were at least as harsh as in the Middle Ages, they were removed from living spaces. They can be carried out in war zones, on an island away from society, etc.

The system, nourished by predispositions influenced by stimuli that seep into the familiar, has gained a quality that can function without external institutions. The "power that has the right to kill" has evolved into "a power that keeps alive and surrounds with health." There is now a power that wins because it keeps it alive. Power has put the body at the centre of society, has seen the necessity of developing the delusion that it protects the body, and has discovered that it has to give its citizens the idea that it has developed the delusion that it protects them and that this is one of the basic building blocks of the system. Foucault describes this transition process as follows:

> Punishment has gradually ceased to be a spectacle. Moreover, everything that sentence could contain as a spectacle has now become a negative signifier. With the disappearance of the ceremonial presentation of punishment, one begins to suspect that the 'final stage' of discipline also has dark relations with the crime. If punishment does not surpass crime in brutality, it at least equals it, accustoming the spectators to the cruelty that it intends to discourage. It shows them the frequency of crimes; it likens the executioner to a villain, the judges to murderers, reverses the roles at the last moment, and the tormented becomes the object of pity and admiration. Beccaria said very early on: 'We see murder, presented to us as a horrible crime, committed in cold blood and without remorse. Public execution is now seen as a furnace where violence is rekindled. (Foucault, 2006, p. 40–41).

One of the factors in the concealment of the execution processes of political criminals condemned to public punishment is the relationship of the subjects with the apparatus of power. Power is now "the power of the people," or at least this discourse is constructed everywhere with the "republic." However, in the West, from the late eighteenth century onwards, many outsiders began to take shelter in the cities. Many cities were divided into two, and the working class and the bourgeoisie settled on both sides of the cities. The masses that could not be fed sufficiently from the system were open to social movements, especially at that time, and were dissatisfied with the dominant paradigm. This mass, consisting of workers, sex workers, vagrants, the unemployed, and the homeless, were victimized by the relations of the wild wheels of capitalism, were left out and formed a tough crowd in the cities. In time, these masses would carry out the European labor movements of 1830, 1848, and 1871 and the great upheavals.

In this environment where the myth of the individual is glorified, the staging of the punishment of the criminal by the representatives of power is contrary to the new structure. From now on, the elements that constitute a crime are examined, and a large army of officials consisting of psychiatrists and lawyers reduce crime to the psychology of the individual by detaching it from society. On the other hand, political crime is marginalized by the same tools, and those who commit these crimes are excluded, especially with the label of "madness." In the same era, there is a glorification of reason, and this label has essential functions not to examine the infrastructure of crime. Because examining the infrastructure of political crime will reveal the reality of human exploitation on which the system is based.

Rather than punishing the individual's body, a group of apparatuses and officials who shape it from the early stages and manage its consciousness have now come into play. Michel Foucault summarizes this situation: "If not the body, then the soul is intervened". The penance that rages the body must be replaced by a penalty that profoundly affects the heart, thought, will, and mental state (Foucault, 2019, p. 50). The historical development of the problem of insanity within the concepts of punishment and crime also confirms these arguments.

Judicial processes are also subject to a series of decisions. The ideological propositions of law, medicine and social sciences reinforce each other and establish a blockade. The fact that their reality is not questioned is an imposition of the structure itself. The state, sanctified in the consciousness of the subjects, and science, universalized under the veil of being impartial even though it is adorned with its ideology, provide the necessary support for this process.

Michel Foucault summarizes the fundamental change in criminal proceedings as follows:

Knowledge of the violation, knowledge of the perpetrator, and knowledge of the law were the three conditions on which a judgment could be based on reality. However, a completely different question of fact is now involved in criminal proceedings. It is no longer a question of 'Has the incident been established, and does it constitute a crime?' but What is this incident? What are this violence and murder? In which sphere of reality should this be included? Is it a daydream, a psychological reaction, or a moment of madness? Is it a moral disorder? It is no longer only 'Who is the perpetrator?' but also 'How should the causal process that brought this about be included? What is the place of the perpetrator in this process? What is the origin? Instinct, unconscious, environment, culture?' It is no longer 'What law sanctions this violation?' but also 'What is the most appropriate solution?' How can the development of the subject be predicted? In what way can they be rehabilitated with the greatest certainty? A judgment of the individual in terms of evaluation, diagnosis, prediction, and rules is embedded in the structure. (Foucault, 2006, p. 54).

Those who judge have become a team, a multidisciplinary oligarchy has formed, and the judicial processes have become complex. Fields such as psychiatry, sociology, etc., were also involved, and universities and judicial processes sometimes acted together. As knowledge about the offender's body and psychology, personal history and the nature of the crime increases, so does the power of the bio-political apparatus. The trial has become a process of joint action by a wider team and a broader power apparatus. Finding the causes of crime and delving into the psychological and sociological processes that prepare crime is not aimed at building a better system. The aim is to establish a perfect system that will not affect the rents and profits of the sovereigns and, within this system, to discipline the subject and make it the most suitable for the system. In the later stages of this phase, social media statistics will come into play, and the economy of desire will be organized much more clearly. It is about using subjects most ergonomically and integrating them into capitalism.

According to Foucault (2006, p. 63), the body is surrounded by power relationships because it is a productive force; however, the body can only be constituted as a labour force in a relationship of subordination. Necessity is also a political tool that is carefully organized, calculated and used. The body can only become a reasonable force when it is productive and subordinated. They can use either violence or ideology to achieve this subordination. It can be direct, the power can be used against force, and it can be directed against material elements, but therefore it can be non-violent. It can be calculated, organized, technically thought out, and subtle. It can resort to neither arms nor terror but remain at the concrete level. Knowledge and domination constitute what can be called the political technology of the body.

The biopower over the body cannot be explained only in terms of controlling the body's activities in production. If presented this way, biopower must be extended to modern times and all times of class society. The use of the body in production was much more intense in pre-modern times. A large part of the subjects of the enslaved state were forced to work much more severely than today. Nevertheless, the body's transformation into a primary consumption issue has yet to be traced back that far. For this to happen, the consumer society and the forest and post Fordist production revolutions that underpinned it had to occur. It also requires the proliferation of mass media and the pumping of consumer culture. If one pillar of biopower is the valorization of the body in the production process, the other is precisely its being the real subject of consumption. The necessity of issues is the main factor in dismembering or destroying the body in punishment and educating it.

What Zizek (2019) calls "phantasmatic supports" are the key points that provide the intensity and inflation of speech, and these phantasmatic supports cling to the desire for self-expression. Fantasy is in opposition to reality. When reality is reached, fantasy disappears. Reality cannot generate so much speech practice. Although it cannot be proved, one can say this: people have never talked so much at any age. Talking is the main element that provides Zizek's "phantasmatic support". "Desire is the wound of reality," says Zizek (2019). Speaking cannot be read independently of our presentation or desire for the self. A universe of speech becomes an effort to reach that phantasmatic self that can never be reached. Since the person, as a poetic being, has to perceive reality through "phantasms", he has produced a machine that mobilizes all the urgency he produces through desire and phantasms. Zizek (2019) attributes libido as a functionality that provides the energy between substances, events and phenomena.

Every reality, especially the human self, is subject to a politics of desire and is constructed through imaginative support. One of the leading constructors of this imaginary support is talking. Speaking ensures the continuity of imaginative support and builds a barrier in front of reality, insecurity and uncertainty. This barrier is so strong that the moments of perceived realization are the rare moments of surprise, dream and unconsciousness. Lacan's placement of woman in the image of man and his radical statement that "there is no woman" can be placed on the whole plane and space. Everything that human beings are in relation with is an imagination, a design and a reflection of the self. Even so-called matter and material relationalities carry fragments of human desire. Speech is constructed through desires precisely to ensure the continuation of these fantasies. Prohibitions such as censorship strengthen these fantasies, which would be one reason why creative and intellectual acts emerge in the most challenging moments, such as absence or revolution. The interrogative and productive power of crisis moments is related to how prohibition and silencing increase internal dynamism.

We can no longer speak of silencing but of the domestication of speech. This is a passive manipulation, thanks to the inflation of discourse. The signifying atmosphere of society had evolved to a different point from the periods when it had to be controlled by the ruling classes. However, social transformations and postmodern life practices, especially since the last quarter of the twentieth century, have begun to break the centrality of this control. Postmodern life practices violently attack every phenomenon centralized and managed by an apparatus.

Deleuze explains in one of his speeches that information and communication are systems of control. Knowledge is to give instructions. Having an opinion is only sometimes about communication, according to Deleuze. The purpose of communication is to disseminate information, a form of instruction. When information is given, it is also an instruction as to what to believe. Information is a set of instructions about what we should believe or appear to believe. In this sense, according to Deleuze, information and communication are a system of control. However, the reason for weakening the external control of speech these days is that it does not convey information. Speech that does not convey instructions indicates a generalized decentralization, lack of instructions, and lack of knowledge. Therefore, there is no need for censorship or control anymore. Because communication has gone beyond the control systems, Deleuze refers to it. It is now only an effort to materialize desire and reveal the imagination of the self. The "disciplinary society" seen in Foucault and initiated by Foucault during the Napoleonic period needed censorship. Because knowledge had to be controlled, today, however, we are moving to a "society of control" where closures are dissolved. From schools to prisons, confinement centres are becoming walled and decentralized. The debates about lockdown centers reveal a certain change in society everywhere. There is no need to ban speech in this social transformation because the system is a collection of controls that have been transformed into a particular legal dimension. In the context of high-speed mobilizations, speech is no longer a distribution of instructions or information but an exchange of desire and a presentation of being. The selves and their images, now constantly presented as an empty resistance to death, reflect the pain of speech to stabilize existence. Constant talking as an effort to stabilize one's being has become the obligatory act of today's imaginary world.

In a period when it becomes increasingly difficult for subjects to get out of control, and even when they do, they feed the dominant paradigm, there is no need for apparatuses. The police are now in the psychic structure of subjects; every subject is a police officer. In such an environment, silencing does not occur through fascist practices as seen in centralized state structures.

Consciousness is already silenced from birth. Even if it breaks it, it cannot find supporters. Aldous Huxley's prophetic society, "The Brave New World," has come true. Although workers are not silenced like enslaved people, they are controlled by the way they address each other by company policies. If the company does not control these forms of address, they will be controlled by society's aristocratic rules of respect. Employees of fast-food companies are obliged to address each other with titles such as sir and madam.

Working conditions prevent a function that enriches vocabulary and leads to alternative ideas. The main factor in this is that the production of material life, as in craft culture, fails to develop the essential qualities of human beings. What Karl Marx referred to as "alienation" results from the fact that life in the workplace also dulls the worker's consciousness. Today, self-activity and the production of material life are so separated that material life is the goal and the production of material life, i.e. work, is the means. The life process of society, which is based on the process of material production, cannot be stripped of the mystical veil that envelops it until the exhibition is consciously organized by people freely assembled and according to a definite plan (Marx, 2007, p. 181). In societies of millions of people working in environments where workplaces have become factories of alienation, there is no longer any need to control speech by coercion. Speech has become automated and mechanized, moving away from thoughtfulness. According to Horkheimer (2005, p. 68), to the extent that thoughts become automated and instrumentalized, they find it difficult to see themselves as meaningful. They are seen as objects, as machines. Discourse has now become one of the tools, a screw in the giant production apparatus of contemporary society.

Every sentence with no function in the giant production apparatus cannot find its place in the world of meaning and loses its value. Even reality will remain accurate and continue to rule to the extent that it can be calculated and find its place in this giant apparatus called a "system". Horkheimer summarizes this situation as follows:

> When a thought or a word becomes a tool, the need to actually 'think' it, i.e. the need for the logical acts that must perform in verbalizing it, disappears. As has often and rightly been pointed out, this 'intellectual economy' is the advantage of mathematics, the model of all neo-positivist thought. Complicated logic operations bypass all the mental acts on which mathematical and logical symbols are based. Such mechanization is indeed necessary for the development of the industry. Still, when it also becomes the chief characteristic of minds, reason becomes instrumentalized, a kind of materiality and blindness, a fetish, a magical entity that is accepted instead of being lived intellectually. (Horkheimer, 2005, p. 69).

Subjects are collectively related to and affect each other. Human beings cannot live alone; they live in groups. However, Postmodern culture strengthens the system it has established by atomizing the human being with the feeling of being alone and lonely, by narcissizing person and glorifying the myth of the individual. Capitalism, which regrouped itself in the second half of the twentieth century thanks to the post Fordist mode of production and overcame crises in favour of a handful of the rich, has directly attacked the bonds between subjects. From family relations to trade unions, capitalism, primarily through neo-liberal policies, has set out to destroy all forms of solidarity that could hinder the system in the production and consumption of capitalism worldwide. The capitalist system, which produces horizontal and vertical inequalities and concentrates capital in specific world regions, requires its evolution and acts with the conscious occupation of the ruling class. Postmodern culture isolates human beings from other human beings.

The spread of the culture of isolation developed well after the neo-liberal policies of the 1980s, and society has turned into a kind of "F Type Prison." Punishment practices are a reflection of the social structure and an indicator of its evolution. It is possible to read the power relations of a society through the punishment practices of that society. For example, crucifixion was one of the punishments applied to prisoners in ancient Rome. Crucifixion is the process of the criminal's death being carried to a height where people can see and watch. Death is theatricalized. It is turned into a spectacle. So what are the qualities of the community formed by a crucifying power? What kind of social structure does crucifixion indicate?

First of all, the crucifying power establishes itself as a supreme power. The subjects that makeup society feel as worthless as possible in front of the power and worship it directly. Those who break with the established hegemony are punished most harshly. No equal relations exist, and everyone's place, societal roles, and class positions are determined. In these unequal relations, everything has to be settled in its place and in a static manner. There is no high-speed fluidity like in today's societies. The criminal can be sacrificed and punished in a spectacle. The punishment for creating fluctuations in the static perception of society is death, a punishment that is considered natural. Otherwise, the fact that a person could be nailed by the wrists and ankles and stretched on a board would invite them to revolt against power.

Moreover, social control mechanisms must function in such a society through a more internalized mechanism. Such a death would be unacceptable without a structure that sanctifies power and excessively legitimizes its class within society. In addition, fear must be constantly generated in society, and power must be displayed its power through demonstrations, which is why punishment practices became theatrical during the Middle Ages.

The cross is the transformation of power into a spectacle. Moreover, bodies have no value since this society does not focus its commercial relations on consumer culture. Most of what the subjects consume is what they produce. Although they carry more than what they make to the market, this market is where commodity relations are still emerging in minimal ties. Hundreds of years are still needed for a structure in which gigantic shopping malls, advertising companies, and city centres turn into dumping grounds for commodities. In a society where the relations of production-consumption have not become gigantic, where the capitalist market has not been formed, there is no need to make people forget death. Death is something that can be exhibited.

The cross is the transformation of power into a spectacle. Moreover, bodies have no value since this society does not focus its commercial relations on consumer culture. What subjects consume is what they produce themselves. In autarchic pre-modern societies, the human body is still only a cog in the wheel of the production mechanism. Even though they carry more than they produce to the market, this market is where commodity relations still emerge in minimal relationships. Hundreds of years are still needed for a structure in which gigantic shopping malls, advertising companies and city centres turn into dumping grounds for commodities. In a society where production-consumption relations have not reached enormous proportions, where the capitalist market has not been formed, there is no need to make people forget death. Death is something that can be exhibited. Cemeteries are not outside living spaces.

On the contrary to forgetting death, death will be constantly preached about, the afterlife will be explained, the power of the government to kill will be shown, and movements against the government will be punished as harshly as possible by displaying them. In a giant shopping mall, consumption can only be accelerated by making us forget death. The cross is also an indication that shopping is small-scale and small-market oriented. In a social structure where consumption relations are an essential part of the cycle of the system, tortures, punishments, death, and cemeteries should be located behind and beyond the spaces where life continues. Death must be removed from life. As the example of the cross shows, the punitive practices of power are indicators of the structure of society.

Today's punishment practices reflect the social structure, just like past practices. F-type prisons, officially known as "F-type high security closed prisons," are high-security prisons defined by the Turkish Criminal Execution Law No. 5275. In these prisons, prisoners are separated from other prisoners and left alone. During their first implementation, they were introduced to the public in the media by claiming that they were spotlessly clean, that their walls had just been painted white and that there was no single mark on them. This system of isolating "criminals" with white borders is controversial in many countries because it violates human rights. Throughout human history, pictures and signs have been representing themselves on the walls of the interior spaces where people have lived. This behavior, which today is seen as a wall poster or a painting, is an expression of the inner world of human beings. A closed space with white walls and no one to talk to drives people crazy.

Although the subjects who make up the society outside are formally different from the inmates of the F-type prison, they are essentially the same in that they are each isolated from society and themselves. The subjects of postmodern society live in isolation from each other. The Type F prison system is a reflection of postmodern society. Today's people need help to make sense of messages, even if they can access them. While a prisoner in a Type F prison is left without messages and is subjected to shaping, a subject trapped in postmodern culture is numbed with excessive messages and is prevented from thinking holistically. Being left alone and isolated in the F-type prison brings similar results to isolation through excessive disinformation. Here, too, the structure of society is read through the practice of punishment.

Exposing people to excessive messages, dragging them to indirect ways of communicating with others in society, such as social media applications, and the increasing dominance of mass media over communication means that their imagination is crossed by power. People need real and touchable relationships. Being isolated from a real human community leads this type of person to a peculiar rebellion. This rebellion ranges from complete isolation to depression and drowning in consumer culture. Moreover, most activities they call entertainment are passive, not active. They think that watching entertainment activities is participation.

Millions of people, unable to determine what they need from over-communication and to be part of the politics of constant desire, fill shopping malls, cafes and restaurants twenty-four hours a day, live connected to computer games and the internet, indulge in the "pleasure" that is the engine of the system to forget their pain and deepen their abysses. People squeezed between glass partitions in workplaces, in "f-type" cells, consume their lives in the unhealthy conditions of offices. Their means of communication are downright unhealthy, yet they seem all too natural and normal to each of them. While the offices isolated by partitions prevent people from communicating healthily, they are similar to the punishment practices produced by the same social structure.

It is not only valid in an intellectual sense that the means of communication lead to isolation. The accolades in a Coke commercial or the "life" on offer are not merely indicators of the evaporation of all that is solid. Capitalism keeps people at a distance from each other. It produces millions who cannot communicate openly, even with those closest to them. Adorno and Horkheimer emphasized that small tellers at the train station or in the bank allow employees to whisper and share little secrets with their colleagues. However, the glass partitions of the modern office, the vast halls where countless employees fit and where both comers and managers can watch, do not allow for private conversations and idleness. Even small whispers are now impossible. These people are isolated within the collective (Adorno and Horkheimer, 2010, p. 293).

The isolated human community in the crowds, their selves pressed and atomized and cut off from other people, entropically dispersed and separated from the mass called community, lost the meaning maps of the old societies and scattered in the places called cities. This society is a prison divided into as many F-type cells as there are people. Today's power is a network of these subjects, forming a network of small networks called human beings. While programmed to define and exist for the subjects, every behaviour and attitude contains a hidden commonality. This commonality ensures the continuation of the legitimized relations of subjects who share different positions in establishing power networks and in the order of interaction, which ensures the cycle of the capitalist economy.

Interpersonal communication, directly influenced by social media and other means of communication, has turned into a state of silence based on self-denial and hiding one's inner qualities from each other. The human always talks but cannot say anything about reality. Humans have perhaps never spoken so much throughout history, but since it has never been so far away, they cannot talk about themselves. There are so many styles because of this inability to tell the truth, open up, and reflect on oneself honestly. Hairstyles, carrying various symbols, being different and reflecting this difference with clothes may express this inability to express oneself. F-type society is a society where speech is silence, movement is inaction, understanding is being dumb, and information is based on producing ignorance. In conclusion, it would be helpful to give more information about the isolation system the government has structured as the "F Type Cell."

From the beginning of the 1970s, the working-class struggle in Germany turned into violent politics. Afraid of the return of fascism, various sectors took up arms and waged war against the government to prevent a repeat of the Nazi experience. The massacres of children in the Vietnam War and many others were reported in the European press, and student movements began to mass. The organizational violence that arose in reaction to the barbarities of capitalist governments mainly affected Germany. Although the system condemns this violence, calling it "terrorist acts," there is a class war, and the lines have become clear. The battle between the proletarians and the ruling classes' armed apparatus escalates daily worldwide. In Germany, a situation resembling a state of emergency in Berlin. The RAF (Red Army Fraction) has intensified its actions and is attacking the officers of the state apparatus of the exploiting class who represent power. It is in these conditions that the "Type F Prison" began. The conditions prepared and applied by the Nazis for political criminals were reproduced. Separating and isolating the prisoner from others is a Nazi practice. However, the German state used the same practice in its fight against the RAF. In this way, the power of the political organization is broken, and political prisoners are cut off from each other.

Karabey, in his book *Silent Death*, says of the F-type cells, "The essence of the system can be summarized as the destruction of the personality of the human being by depriving his emotional perceptions of stimuli, the outside world and everything natural, and the imposition of other desired norms in its place" (Karabey, 2001, p. 7). It is essential to pay attention to the following statement: "the depersonalization of human emotional perceptions by depriving them of stimuli, the outside world and all that is natural". Let us highlight the three deprivations described in this statement: "withdrawal from stimuli, the outside world and everything natural". The main reason we conceptualize postmodern society as an F-type society is that society has these three deprivations, albeit in different forms and proportions. Just as the prisoner living in isolation in F-type cells needs these three deprivations, the people of postmodern society experience the same deprivations.

The stimuli circulating in the atmosphere of society are primarily meaningless to subjects, and the number of meaningless messages far exceeds the number that have meaning. This case would lead to a chaotic atmosphere of messages and to conscious confinement to narrow islands of meaning. In postmodern society, every human being is left without vast knowledge and ignorant of many points outside their subject matter. Rising fascism and religious fundamentalism are related to this situation. The refuge of people of past societies in metaphysics evolved and changed form. Today's people also cling to fundamentalism and nationalism and more radically to their small islands of thought in a world they cannot understand. Ignorance is overcome by trusting those with degrees and submitting to authorities. The abundance of messages is as big a problem as the absence of messages. Both are great deprivations for human beings. However, the daily decrease in meaningful messages in the abundance of messages brings an excellent noise to society. Thanks to this increase in noise, the "Type F Society" of postmodern culture will be completed after a while because the abundance of messages and the disconnection of messages from meaning is as terrible as silence.

Terminating their contact with the outside world is another deprivation in the "F Type Cell" model. Political prisoners can see even their first-degree relatives much less than other prisoners, and their isolation is tightened. In this respect, the punishment model resembles the society in which it exists. Postmodern society continues to attack all forms of coexistence, including family relationships. People's desire to live together is weakened by glorifying individual life and solitude.

Also, spatially, postmodern subjects are often confined to a small space. Studio houses are becoming popular, and living alone is becoming more attractive. Subjects imprisoned in the triangle of home-work-shopping center live without being aware of their cells. People in postmodern culture have freedom of movement but lack the conditions and cognitive state to realize it. Moreover, when we consider that communication between people breaks down, especially towards middle age, and that the spaces where people can present themselves as natural and exist are narrowing, it can be understood that relations with the outside world are coming to an end and that these relations are only formal. The relationship is more instrumental and based on the principle of reciprocity than ever before.

All this shows that today's society deserves to be conceptualized as an F-type society. Hüseyin Karabey, who has researched F-type cells in Turkey, documented and published a book on the subject, states that people in these cells are constantly changing prisons and that this is a policy to increase the conditions of isolation:

> When I met a Basque political prisoner who had spent a long time in French prisons, I asked him about these suicides. He said this: When prisoners get depressed because of isolation, the prison administration gives them antidepressive drugs. The prison administration transfers the prisoners to another prison once a year; this is part of the isolation practice. In this way, they prevent any possible social contact. Medication given to prisoners after must resume this transfer after several bureaucratic procedures are completed to have the medication restored. It is during this period that suicides are most common. This is why political prisoners never take medication. The fact that continued the practice despite the knowledge of what it was leading to shows that it was in a sense a murder, but a very clever serial murder. (Karabey, 2001, p. 9).

Among the prisoners interviewed in Karabey's book, Pierino Matta's testimony is riveting. Matta is a prisoner released from the F-type cell, where he spent 23 years due to severe health problems. When asked to describe solitary confinement in one word, he gave the following answer, which, when considered in parallel with the positioning of subjects in society, may sound very familiar to people engaged in postmodern life practices:

> Isolation! You can't describe it in one word because isolation is everything. It is both one thing and everything that affects each other. That's why you can't define isolation with one word. Isolation is everything. You are in prison, not only because you are in prison but also because of everything else that happens there. The fact that... Well... For example... isolation... as I just said... (here he chokes, gets angry, and explodes), isolation is context, and isolation is similarity. It's being beaten. I am not seeing anyone. That's what isolation is. Isolation is not

such a small and simple thing... Isolation also means being isolated from
the sun. A 7-meter wall is built in front of you. Isolation is being unable
to see the sun because of the grates and the wall. Isolation is depriving
me of the sun. It is depriving me of grass, depriving me of everything.
Isolation includes everything, so you cannot define it in two words!
Isolation is imposed on society as a model. (Karabey, 2001, p. 181).

Pierino Matta lived 23 years in the harsh conditions of an F-type cell. What he
describes is very similar to the practices of so-called everyday life. While the
conditions in the workplace often prevented the subjects from seeing the sun and
interacting with nature, modern and post-modern life prevented them from
stepping on the grass. The 7-meter wall he mentions is not foreign to today's subject
when the spaces that make up his life are noticed. In a Jean Baudrillard-like
analysis, we are beings in the delusion of nature, from our food to the trees in the
parks. As Matthew so rightly emphasizes, isolation is a model imposed on society.

The isolation Matthew describes is, in addition to all this, the lack of people
around to talk to. However, in an environment where all sentences are
influenced by social media phenomena and visual message inflation exceeds
the words used, what is the difference between this and isolation if one cannot
have a qualified conversation in a "normal" life? Speaking within the alienating
communication practices of society is worse than being silenced or silenced. In
some Christian sects, the "fast of silence" is a formative act enabling
introspection. However, being in a completely alienating communication
environment leads to the normalization of a much more significant lack, and
this lack becomes the raw energy of the consumer society. This is one of the
sources of the constantly felt emptiness and the reinforcing power of the
Lacanian "*obje petit a*": Talking all the time and not saying anything.

Society has turned into a Prozac® society, and the enormous increase in the
number of depression patients is similar to the high incidence of depression
among criminals in F-type cells (Karabey, 2001, p. 187). In addition, the person
of postmodern society is rootless. It cannot take root spatially. They have to
migrate due to work conditions. Continuous migration increases experience,
overloads memory, and destroys the thousands of years of traditional relations
between geography and people. In postmodern society, speed and constant
movement bring about a kind of amnesia society.

The media forms a particular perception of the world of economically and
culturally marginalized segments of society. This perception, created primarily
through television, newspapers, and social media messages, reshapes their life
practices in the minds of the masses, detached from the reality of these people.
Because the exclusion of these groups from economic relations also limits their
contribution to the dominant paradigm of society. As Bourdieu points out,

those disadvantaged in terms of cultural equipment do not have the right to speak out about political and economic problems; moreover, their lack of the necessary equipment to speak out reinforces their subordinate position and never allows them to speak about their own lives. Only elites in positions of power can talk about their lives and problems; they think and define their problems for them and propose solutions. In short, the media reproduces unequal power relations while further silencing the voiceless (İnal, 2010, p. 37).

The transformation of one's inner world into a space of isolation stems not from the silencing of individuals but from the impulses of narcissistic speech practices. The human being who constantly speaks with the pronoun "I" and describes himself is, in a sense, in a state of searching and never actually producing that "I." Running from message to message in digital media networks, humans hate absolute silence, and loneliness pushes them on a difficult path. Digital networks are the enemy of silence. Reaching an understanding requires silence and depth, a reason why the digital world needs more depth.

Lack of depth leads to speech inflation and produces a narcissistic "I" speech. People wait their turn in conversations and listen to the other person with sparse attention. Reading books is boring, deepening and teaches listening. To read a book is to enter isolation and to be content with it. Digital media is crowded, isolating, and shallow. Digital media does not prevent one from shutting up and allows one to join the crowd's conversation.

In "Vom Verschwinden der Tituale: Eine Topologie der Gegenwart," Byung-Chul Han argues that silence and silence do not find a place in digital media, which requires shallow attention, and that digital communication networks proceed in a flat shallowness, nothing is explained in depth and do not provide intensive information. According to Han, people are urged to communicate powerfully because they have lost silence (Han, 2023, p. 46).

Silence cannot merge with the economy, be sold, or be included in a rapid commodity cycle. The compulsion to produce and the compulsion to communicate go hand in hand and are integrated. Every product must join the sound world glued to a word and take its place in everyday speech practices. Advertising jingles reproduce an anthropological structure by carrying the repetitive anonymous structure of oral culture to the present day, and they complete the communication imperative. The communication noise of digital media shatters the sacredness of "Temmuz," the tree of life in Mesopotamia, and the "Ahlat tree" of Anatolia, which requires silence. Silence walks with the sacred. The communication compulsion of the digital media and the world that turns everything into a product disperses the archetypes imposed by anthropology.

Digital media produce much more discourse than mass media. Since the last century, every new technology has been designed to increase address. The relationship between speech and environmental factors was explained at the beginning. In an environment where noise envelops the world, speech joins the noise. In a sense, this is the death of speech. Everything is added to the noise, and the noise swallows everything. It is impossible to go on a journey of discovery in the noise. Perhaps this is what kills philosophy and literature. Maybe this made Witgeinstein say, "From now on, one must keep silent." The inflation of ideas is the gravedigger of speech, and this is an age in which noise is ideas.

Noise has also been used against truth throughout history. Ideas contrary to the order can also be suppressed by the noise consciously produced by the system. Noise has been used to silence the voice of truth. When the prophet Muhammad began to utter his first verses against the Meccan order, his opponents, who wanted to preserve the order, made noise when he spoke. They tried to drown out his speech with noise. Noise is the opposite of the truth in every respect. Over time, however, this opposition has become confused, and the fact has become increasingly obscured by noise. Today, a scientific debate or an artistic activity sounds very weak. In every age, truth and falsehood have been mixed. But what distinguishes this age is that the fake can successfully imitate the real.

According to Jean Baudrillard, the Second World War was a significant turning point in the formation of the simulation universe. Indeed, after the war, the redrawing of the map of Europe, the emergence of new laws controlling fascism, and the superstructure change required for the system to regroup itself entered an intense phase. In the aftermath of the Second World War, the political alignments of right-wing parties in many countries shifted towards the values of the left values. Technologies developed before the war found market areas and became widespread with the new changes in the world. For example, the spread and diffusion of television worldwide coincided with the years after the Second World War. Likewise, the service sector expanded as much as other industries and reached a level to compete with the giant industries that preceded it. Henceforth, subjects' perception of the world consists of images, and images and images rather than reality dominate the world. Thanks to simulacra, reality has been replaced by images, signs, and codes. In the most general sense, the simulacrum is the established reality perceived as reality. The dominance of hyper-reality is spreading rapidly, and the whole world is turning into deserts of fact where we cannot find the truth, and the simulation universe is formed. Baudrillard defines this universe as follows:

It is the state of hyper-reality, which is devoid of an origin, which symbolizes the derivation of reality through models, the state of 'pretending' that something or a situation that really and exists, with all its components, is real and exists. (Baudrillard, 2005, p. 103).

According to Byung Chul-Han (2022b, p. 54), there is a communication crisis; thought requires silence. Interpretations that adapt to the unusual noise caused by new means of communication continue at the very heart of digital media. Commenting on the image speaks to another viewer, and millions of conversations every day, combined with the idea, only serve to discharge and sink further into the pit of positioning the image. Commenting on the image and talking to other viewers is like the cry of people lost in the mass. Speaking to the audience through the image, which has become a gambling indulgence, is the cry of lost subjects who cannot exist and cannot even dream anymore in the hope of being able to live. These screams, "dopamine mania," are among the most obvious signs of people's loneliness in crowds.

When speech finds an audience, dopamine is released from the brain to maintain communication. Nature wants us to socialize. Talking and talking to someone else gives pleasure. Humans, social beings, enjoy communicating; that's the basis of interactive communication. Phones, the most prominent interactive communication tool, have become little dopamine boxes, and images fill the entire consciousness. Images produce fantasies and dreams instead of people. In a world occupied by appearances, it is impossible to dream anymore because those who long for you are at your fingertips.

Chapter 5

Self-Censorship: Human is Being Doomed to Remain Silent as They Become Civilized

Quiet! Quiet! In the cool air, when everything in your heart is calm, you can hear some things you couldn't hear during the day.

Now it speaks, is heard, and stalks the hearts that spend the night awake; ah! Oh, how he sighs! How he laughs in his dreams!

Do you not hear how secretly, horribly, sincerely he speaks to you, that ancient, deep, deep midnight?

Oh man, give ear!

(Nietzsche, 2013, p. 326)

Humans are highly complex creatures intellectually, intuitively, and emotionally. Ever since they refused to be an animal, they have rejected all kinds of instincts and thus their nature; they have shaped their whole life through this rejection and has been rendered incapable of reflecting this complexity outwardly, thanks to the power mechanisms to which they are subjected. The times when a person communicates with itself the most and realizes its inner communication is getting shorter by the day. In Friedrich Nietzsche's novel *Böyle Buyurdu Zarathustra* (Thus Spake Zarathustra), he expresses, "I sat in solitude for a long time, I forgot to be silent." He has moved away from that intense inner communication because he is connected to other channels with people in the outside world and the messages he receives from the outside world. In a sense, the more they speak, the more they are condemned to silence, and the reason why they say this is to hide what is real, the reality that they cannot confess even to themselves and cannot reach their awareness. Jean-Paul Sartre, who saw this reality, expressed this reality in an interview with Michel Contat when he was 70 years old as follows:

I don't give you my subjectivity, I don't give it to anyone, because I have a dark depth that refuses to be told even to me, that I can say to myself, but that denies to be related to anyone else even to me. (Contat, 1996, p. 19)

It is not implausible that we talk to escape from that deep point that Sartre discusses, or instead, that this is why we talk so much. It is impossible to measure, but it is quite possible to argue that the subjects of no society before ours spoke so much. Just as Arthur Schopenhauer said that consciousness is a structure built to cover up the futility of life, talking can be another way of covering up human meaninglessness. As psychoanalysis reveals, speaking can tell part of our inner self. Halil Cibran puts it this way:

> When you speak, you stop being at peace with your thoughts. And when you can no longer remain in the desolation of your heart, you start living with your lips. The voice becomes, for you, a pastime, a means of passing the time. And in most of your speeches, thought is half slaughtered; thought is like a bird flying in the void; in the cage of words, it can take wing, but it cannot fly. (Cibran, 2021, p. 179)

Unless one has mastered meditation techniques, the moment one begins to speak, one experiences a relative detachment from one's inner dynamics. Like Cibran and Sartre, Soren Kierkegaard emphasizes the deeper meanings hidden in the speech by saying, "The sharpest of silences is not silence but speech." Albert Camus reiterates that address contains much more sense than it expresses and that there is a meaning that cannot be said:

> Deep emotions, like great works, always carry more meaning than what they consciously say. The continuity of a movement or a hatred in a soul is also seen in habits of doing or thinking; it goes on and on with consequences unknown even to the soul itself. (Camus, 2012, p. 29).

Language tends to escape from its signified richness of representation. Through the organization and associations between words, it can contain multiple signifiers at the same time. Despite this unity, it also has more than it communicates. A language that can speak is more than just a language. Language can interpret part of that excess, that which is immanent in and transcends objects. However, it cannot directly reveal this transcendence. Because ultimately, things remain unknowable. Everything perceived as "the external world" finally carries an interiority. In a sense, subjects are imprisoned in their discourses and are influenced by their discourses to perceive the lessons of others. However, all this cannot change the following fact. The world is built on a series of material resistances and conflicts. How one perceives the world does not change this fact.

Communication between people has become a miscommunication as society has become more complex, and roles and statuses have become a veil that obscures human reality. Charles Baudelaire expresses this situation in a meaningful century. The eighteenth-century city of Paris is a city that has the dispositives to make this description, and the human being has now lost himself in large crowds and succumbed to the mass:

> The world survives only on misunderstandings. People reconcile with each other as a result of a universal misunderstanding. For if they had understood each other in the past, they would never have reconciled. (Naz, 1997, p. 147).

As Baudelaire put it, if people could communicate with each other more intimately, or if they had a way of communicating that would allow them to understand each other, it would reveal what the capitalist system has done to human beings. It shows what wounded animal humans are hiding behind sterile masks, with who knows what brutal practices, and venting their spleen.

Where does the urge to speak come from? Other than communicating and organizing to survive, what are the impulses that drive people to say? Is one of the impulses that drive people to speak the subconscious mechanisms of being in an unprotected world?

The ego must harmonize all kinds of blind passions arising from the unconscious with the criteria and facts that society constructs as reality. By satisfying these blind passions of the unconscious, the ego keeps the subject in the position of necessity. According to Charrier, it is expressed in conscious activities (perception, speech, mental processes) and allows for the control of the articulation of motor and verbal expressions. It adjusts the personality to the environment and harmonizes the opposing demands of reactions and social imperatives (Charrier, 2020, p. 45). Undoubtedly, the language we speak bears traces of unconscious structures. A dialectical relationship exists between the cold and language system, not a one-sided relationship. As a result, symptoms and symbols are often selected based on a person's language structure.

On the other hand, it is necessary to ask whether the unconscious structures are structured like a language because the unconscious manifests itself precisely only in discourse-related behavior, so much so that the coherent meanings of the symbolic associative chain reach the level of whole meaning only by registering at the level of verbal behavior (Charrier, 2020, p. 108).

Zijderveld, describing language acquisition after human birth, says that in the primary acculturation stage, the baby pays attention to the meanings it quickly observes around the crib. A smile means closeness, kissing expresses affection, and regular feeding and cleaning are signs of parental care and attention. The gestures, movements, sounds, and words around the crib all point to something that transcends the purely mechanical and physiological – the world of the senses (closeness, love, care) and values (happiness and life).

The baby quickly learns that this symbolic world is pleasant and can be reached through its efforts. The most important thing the baby experiences is the realization that most throat sounds are more than air vibrations. Sounds have meaning; they express something, and words form sentences. Thus, language emerges. The young child enters into the process by actively participating. First with funny language games that only imitate sounds, then with actual words, and finally with sentences (Zijderveld, 2022, p. 165).

Even the most minor child knows creaturely that it is completely unprotected. There is evidence that human beings are never – potentially – free of this fear and that these fears are reactivated in environments of oppression. Is speech an antidote to the meaninglessness of existence and the greatest fear of existence: loneliness? Subjects are constantly organized to conceal the fact that they are completely unprotected. People in the wild organized themselves out of fear of nature and came together to fight it and increase their survival ability. However, postmodern subjects choose to talk as a way out of the cages they have built for themselves. Whatever they talk about, this is seen as a practice of liberation for them, of asserting their existence.

There will always be something one cannot tell, which is an existential quality of the human being. In addition to being unable to express what is in its consciousness due to social pressure, there is always a part of the subject that itself cannot realize, that it cannot confess even to itself. When Friedrich Nietzsche said, "What you think you are born not the slightest resemblance to what you are" (Nietzsche, 2009, p. 60), he expressed something relevant to this discussion.

Humans are doomed to remain silent, unable to express themselves in all aspects. A human is a being who speaks to hide intentions. It sinks into the swamp of words to define existence, and the more the inner world is expressed, the more it gets stuck in obscurity. This condemnation stems from the fact that humans cannot always express their thoughts and feelings and are under pressure at this very point, under all circumstances. Human beings, a species that accepts to live with the community and can never live alone, have had to limit their expressions and increase their possibilities of adaptation to conform to the morality of the sovereign to ensure their ability to survive in the community. The expansion of capitalism and the tightening of the bureaucratic walls often mentioned by Max Weber – what Weber calls the "Iron Cage" – has further reinforced man's deficiency. Human condemnation to remain silent is the factor underlying many artistic activities.

Despite breaking many walls to express everything, there are still many impulses that he is unaware of, that are structured in his subconscious, which were instrumental in constructing the subject. This act of expression will surely hit a wall. The state of silence or being silenced mentioned above also contains a dialectic. The inner world of the silenced is more prosperous and more developed. For a large part of the history of civilization, the male is much more comfortable in this regard than the other genders. Perhaps because of this comfort and power of discourse, he has become a flatter and more incomplete creature towards life. The other genders are much more artistic and can think from different angles than males. If a mind is not masculinized, it has this breadth and richness.

Luce Irigaray (2006) attributes women's inability to speak to the masculinization of language. A patriarchal civilization has devalued the feminine to such an extent that their picture of the world is inaccurate. Therefore, instead of continuing to exist as distinct in language, the feminine has become a non-masculine, in other words, an abstract reality that does not exist. In the same way, a woman finds herself confined to the sexual sphere; the feminine grammatical genre has been perceived and destroyed as a subjective and personalized expression, which would be why women have such difficulty speaking and being heard as women. Women have been excluded and ignored by the patriarchal linguistic order. Therefore, from a patriarchal perspective it would be impossible to be a woman and speak coherently and rationally. This cruel situation about discourse could lead to the withdrawal of most women who want to talk culturally from a position they imagine to be neutral. In such a position, women are forced to deny their gender and their species (Irigaray, 2006, p. 19).

Although thought and speech are supposed to correspond, addresses cannot reach the richness of thought. Maurice Blanchot expresses this: "Although thought and speech are believed to communicate, the lesson cannot get the richness of thought." Blanchot describes this situation as follows: "Indeed, 'I think leads to the unmistakable certainty of the I and its existence,' whereas 'I speak' retracts this existence, disperses it, erases it, and allows only its empty place to appear" (Blanchot, 2005, p. 13).

The feeling of inadequacy is an impulse that permeates subjects living in modern and post-modern times. This feeling, one of the basic impulses that provide capitalism with its driving force, stems from the fact that issues question themselves and consistently fail to adapt to the functionalities imposed on them by the system. However, human beings are already inclined to rebel against what capitalism imposes. The problem is ultimately not in itself but in the attempt to put it into certain molds. Blanchot writes, "The consciousness of inadequacy arises when a consciousness cannot realize itself without the other" (Blanchot, 1997, p. 15). The consciousness of inadequacy is necessary for subjects to speak and realize themselves through speaking. Since the consciousness of the inadequacy of issues increases as capitalist relations increase, today's people are constantly talking about themselves. They begin their sentences with "I" to declare their existence to another person and assert themselves as beings. This has become the fate of subjects who cannot achieve what they produce or cannot be satisfied with what they make, in short, who cannot realize themselves.

Signs do not reveal the thought in their nakedness, and there will always be a gap between them. Cannot think of the image, but it can serve as a sign, or rather, it can coexist with the thought in character; it can respect the place that thought will occupy in the future; while it has not yet appeared, it can reveal its peripheral lines while it is still absent. The image is a frozen thing, always dependent on the act of consciousness that accompanies it. Still, the sign and the signified image are capable of change, even if, for the time being, they are without implication, that is, far from being able to establish continuous and theoretically unlimited relations with other entities of the same type (this is the prerogative of the concept).

The ordinary reality of human beings is a veil that covers their traumatic existence, and one of the most prominent elements of this veil is speech. By speaking, humans escape their traumatic reality and, in a sense, move away from themselves. From a Lacanian point of view, speech is one of the most apparent indicators of human escapism, as in the case of "the dream being more real than reality."

In the oldest mythologies of humanity, these stories are symbolic. For example, the "ney," one of the oldest instruments of Mesopotamia, was first used by the Sumerians in Mesopotamia. The oldest finding of this instrument, believed to have been used in Sumerian society around 5000 B.C., is the "ney" dating from 3000–2800 B.C., which is now on display at the Philadelphia University Museum in the United States. An ancient legend about the "ney" instrument, played today in Turkey, Iran, and Arab countries, explains the internal mechanisms of speech.

According to legend, the prophet Muhammad could not bear to keep the secrets that Allah had told him and entrusted them to his close friend Ali, who was very advanced in mystical eastern sciences:

–Don't reveal these secrets!

Ali could not bear these secrets told to him; he could not tolerate them and was trapped under them. He falls into the desert. He pours the mystery he hid inside into a deep well. Over time, the well overflows with water. This overflowing water turns the well into a reed bed, and reeds and reeds grow around it. Realizing that these reeds make pleasant sounds in the wind, a shepherd cuts one of them and makes a "Ney" out of it. But the sound emanating from the Ney is so sincere and deep that everyone becomes enamored of its deep, soulful, and searing melody. They cry with it and start laughing with it. The shepherd's fame soon spread, and Arab tribes began to play this instrument (Topbaş, 2005).

In the history of all kinds of superstructural institutions, from art history to the history of religions and mythology, it is possible to see traces of a counter stance related to revealing inner silence. The exceptional is shut down and suppressed as much as possible. The sovereign defines the exception that creates the space where it is possible to trace the boundaries between inside and outside and where it can assign specific rules to certain areas. Just as here, it is the only language, as something stripped of all concrete instances of speech, with the potential to signify and symbolize, that distinguishes the linguistic from the non-linguistic and creates meaningful spheres of discourse where specific terms correspond to particular meanings. In a state of perpetual exception, language is the sovereign, which declares that nothing is outside language and that language always transcends itself.

A sine qua non-condition for the continuation of the structure and the legitimization by various means of the ruling classes' maximum interest from surplus value is to make the masses accept that this is the natural right of the ruling class. For this, controlling the discourse of the oppressed is functional. Discourses and common representations produce this justification. State apparatuses need to be able to fulfill their supervisory function perfectly. Any institution cannot entirely control addresses. Humans are coded to say "no" due to their existential conditions. He is curious, and his coding to expand his limits is embodied in the word "No." Although the urge to expand its boundaries may seem like a mechanism that works to the detriment of society thanks to capitalism, as in the case of imperialism, in the end, humans are responsible for breaking their chains to a great extent, and institutions cannot fully control this.

The urge to transform is slower in other living beings other than humans. All activities towards this end are instinctive in other creatures. Transformation, which perhaps still dominates human beings even if they lose their instincts, which is the case in every living being connected to nature, is a requirement of the laws of evolution. Human beings, which are not creatures that act only instinctively due to the laws of development, may have entered a flawed evolutionary process due to the alienation brought about by their detachment from nature. This loss of instinct underlies the concept of desire. As human instincts atrophy, these existential concerns have permeated all activities based on expressions, such as speech and art.

The needs for security and transformation are conflicting concepts. Security is the gateway to stability; transformation is the gateway to uncertainty and risk. Both are subject to the general law of dialectic processes: they feed on each other and are intertwined. Communication, and therefore speech as a communicative activity, is an indispensable apparatus for both needs. The ruling classes rely on security to preserve the standard of living the system offers them.

On the other hand, the oppressed are always inclined to transform. The production of consent and, when necessary, repression is essential for this inclination to be tempered. The ruling class knows this very well. Any excavation into the depths of the social dimension of silencing reveals this building block.

The accounts of the lives of the prophets are compelling examples, even if it is not anthropologically sure that they lived. The persecution Moses, Buddha, and Mohammed faced in spreading their teachings is nothing compared to the persecution faced by Jesus. This is because the other three revolutionaries belonged to the ruling classes of the society in which they spread their teachings. As a carpenter, Jesus realized the oppression of the power he held as he awoke. While others experienced an awakening brought about by existential concerns and belonging to the ruling class, Jesus is a revolutionary who is closer to the life practices of the oppressed. Of course, he rebelled against the dominant paradigm of his society, a metaphysical paradigm. This was the mental structure of this time. This rebellion ended in a way unique to its class: Torture and Execution. Violence was used to suppress the uprising of the oppressed at that time. As a result of the consumer society, Jesus spoke at a time when concepts such as "social democracy" and "human rights" were not yet needed. His followers suffered great persecution after him. In Anatolia, refuges are built in regions such as Cappadocia and Kilistra, which were established because of Roman exploitation. It was only when interpretations of his ideas were transformed that they became the general paradigm. Meetings such as the Council of Nicaea exemplify this transformation process. Some 300 years later, Jesus' ideas were accepted by the rulers. Not in their original form, of course. The transformation of Jesus' ideas in the councils is similar to the adaptation of Marx's ideas to social democracy. Revolutionary discourses are transformed into a form suitable for the system.

As the narrative shows, silencing has not always been and cannot always result from repression. The main thing is the production of consent, persuasion, and the development of activities aimed at effectiveness, in other words, legitimization. The process of bending and twisting discourse and integrating it into a system. It is the ability to assimilate even the staunchest dissidents and opponents. The ruling classes learn this lesson from history and continue to exploit it.

What is in question now is the "self-exploitation" internalized by the "society of achievement," as Byung Chul Han puts it. Subjects who are entrepreneurs and lead a life based on performance are simultaneously perpetrators and victims, reflected in language as can/may. From a disciplinary society equipped with should/should, we have moved to a society of skill (Chul-Han, 2022a, p. 17). In the "can/can do" society dominated by words ending with -may, the subject who exploits himself is much more of an enslaved person than the subject used by the boss (Chul-Han, 2022b). A life based on being able to do the subject into a thousand pieces creates a high-tension domination. It now understands freedom as "the freedom to do", which leads to a consciousness that begins all conversations with "I" to subjects who walk to the center of the world but struggle because they cannot be this center. The lack of distance makes every desire for intimacy with another subject, with another, impossible. With digital media terminating distance, it is an excellent hell that everyone is so far apart.

It was, however, a process that created the state apparatuses and the entire superstructure that led to the domestication of speech. Foucault emphasizes that power has domesticated discourse, composed of cells, including state apparatuses, which are all-encompassing and interact. Capitalist activities associated with commodity production and rapid change have shaped society's way of life and relations, and in such an environment, speech has lost its richness. In a sense, all forms of expression, including art, have been detached from their context of meaning. Being easily consumable has infiltrated the world of human purpose. As Karl Marx showed in his work, the commodity form and the question of the value of the commodity in bourgeois society is the cell of capitalist societies.

Chapter 6

The Evolution of the Speech into a
Counter-Revolutionary Structure

We are immersed in a universe full of useless words, where questions and answers are equivalent.

E. M. Cioran (2012, p. 27)

Many philosophers, both idealists and materialists, have addressed the problem of human alienation. While Farabi and Ibn-i Sina questioned that separation from the essence, which they defined as "Wajibü-l Vücud" and whose existence is necessary, would cause alienation, Georg Wilhelm Friedrich Hegel found the cause of separation in a spiritual rupture. Karl Marx is the thinker who explains alienation with worldly data in a materialist cause-effect relationship. Marx processes parting on three primary axes.

First, it is the worker's position in the production process, which is still the general situation of the working masses today. According to Marx (2007), the object produced by labor, its product, resists it as a foreign entity, a power independent of the producer. Work development is labor determined in an object, labor embodied in a thing, and the objectification of labor. The realization of delivery is its objectification. In the sphere of political economy, this realization of work is seen as the loss of reality for the worker, objectification as the loss of the object or slavery to the thing, and appropriation as alienation and deprivation. Marx believed that capitalism conceals the separation caused by the unmediated relation between worker and production and legitimizes it through various interpretations provided by social structures. While alienated labor extracts the worker from the product, it also takes away human qualities in a hidden way. Marx's statement in the 1844 Manuscripts that "the more the worker produces, the more impoverished he becomes" should not be taken as purely economic impoverishment. This impoverishment is also the impoverishment of humanity and realism.

The second is the alienation created by monetary relations, which persists in postmodern times. "A currency-based monetary system in which all values are measured in money results in the independence of the social character of things, about all individuals, and the activity of commerce, which is based on alienation, in the total production and exchange relations, which appear in every individual, in every individual, seeming to bind each individual to itself"

(Marx, 2007, p. 114). Money, the symbol on which relations of production and exchange are based, infects every phenomenon and all human relations in capitalist society. Thus, every type of relationship finds meaning through monetary value, alienating human beings from their essence/nature.

The third concept we will introduce while summarizing Karl Marx's concept of alienation is commodity fetishism. Production and exchange relations revolve around commodities. In addition to its use value, the item has an exchange value. Use value is the value of a thing arising from need. On the other hand, exchange value is determined by political economy and is entirely defined in capitalist relations. The transformation of the commodity into a mysterious object, in other words, commodity fetishism, is another factor of alienation. According to Marx (2004b, p. 82), there is no absolute connection between the existence of commodities and the relation of value between the products of labor that mark them as commodities and their physical properties and the material relations arising from them. According to him, the social connection between people forms an imaginary link between things. "The fact that commodities are shrouded in a specific mystery, and their exchange value increases thanks to this mystery creates a surreal value sequence in the socio-economic paradigm it produces, thus exacerbating alienation."

In his work *Reification or the Anxiety of Late Capitalism*, Timothy Bewes argues that alienation results from the fact that humanity's arrogance, which increases as the Tower of Babel rises, is punished by the fragmentation of the only language they use between them into different world languages, thus forever severing the connection between the world of words and the world of objects and phenomena. This rupture is the necessity realized in another religious myth, the expulsion of Adam and Eve from the Garden of Eden and, in a sense, their separation from reality (Bewes, 2008).

Carl Gustav Jung (2022) argues in his work "Orientation to the Human Spirit" that human consciousness consists of four essential elements. The intensity of these elements, which can be divided into sensation, thought, intuition, and emotion, varies from person to person. Of course, each of the four elements is present in the person. But intensifying one of these elements affects the person's psychological structure. For example, "When emotion reaches a dangerous level, it means that emotion does not assume the function of harmony and keeps the individual under its sovereignty" (Jung, 2022, p. 89). When postmodern life is observed, we will see that its most significant impact on subjects causes actions aimed at increasing emotion. Television mediums', which has become widespread worldwide after the Second World War, occupy a large part of human beings' time. Many of those messages appeal to various emotions and even continuously load emotions. While the news has a network of messages woven with feelings of hatred or pity rather than questioning qualities,

TV series or television movies lead to a catharsis-based opiate rather than making us think. While the constant pursuit of visual messages causes scattered thoughts and difficulty concentrating when silent, subjects can only gather their emotions and get away from their ideas when speaking. As such, the inability to speak and be alone is now a de facto/essential position for the postmodern subject. This new type of human being, who cannot withstand the euphoria at the limits of consciousness when silent or who instinctively senses that he can reach these limits, continues the trance cries of primitives while awake. Trance cries have become the daily speech of postmodern subjects. Ecstatic cries are distortions that are difficult to control by the self. They do not accept the social order, and while they ensure the personal postmodernization of the subject, in other words, the distorted rule-breaking and emancipation (!), dragging more and more towards collective psychosis. Carl Gustav Jung said that the only way to suppress the euphoric effect is to escape it. Today's people are not thirsty because they desire to escape their euphoric influences.

Since time immemorial, rulers have understood the necessity of controlling speech and its power in organizing. One of the most significant indicators is the legend of the Tower of Babel in the Torah. According to the Legend of the Tower of Babel in the Torah, God, thinking that if all humanity spoke the same language, they would be overcome with arrogance and greatness, disrupted their speech and unity, scattered people from Babel to different places, and wanted them to speak different languages in different areas and not understand each other. According to the same legend, God punished humanity because humankind might rise and rebel against God while speaking a common language (Aytaç, 2005).

The speech is inherently dialectical, and repression is one aspect of this debate. An internal impulse is translated into symbols after being shaped by an external embodiment. These embodiments are numerous, from frictions that cause vibrations that produce sounds to pressures brought about by the structure itself, the apparatus of the system, or by a third party other than the subject.

Although speech contains freedom, it constantly carries an antagonism within itself because language is the building block of power. The diversity of the speakers is the main element that feeds speech, and in this context, speech draws a parallel path with freedom as it provides this diversity. However, every power acts to establish control over the word in circulation. For power to be functionalized, the speech used by the sovereign must be, and is, much more potent than the speech used by the oppressed. The monarch's speech may contain the violence inherent in power, but it may also be based on producing the consent of its subjects. The ideological discourse that makes command or consent is constantly repeated on the oppressed. During the order, power is often explicitly revealed. However, during the production of licenses through ideological discourses, they are hidden behind symbols. Strength does not always act through coercion, as in the sign of God in the Babylonian myth. It infiltrates discourses more subtly and constructs its interpretation of the material world from the ground up. To maintain the rule of the sovereign, the subjects' silence, or their interpretation of the world, as if they led the conversation, is essential.

Tzevetan Todorov (2008) says, "The self is someone else". According to Todorov, what constitutes a person is the images they acquire from other people in the community in which they live, and the word is one of the most important of these images. The word that separates the other from oneself is not impermeable. Others not only exist spontaneously around us; they are internalized from the youngest age, making images part of the human being. A person's interiority shares qualities with the interiority of those around them, and the intensity of those qualities reinforces the ideology of the system. In this sense, to control speech and other images is to control human existence.

The inseparability of language and ideology places the responsibility for being buried under a mass of useless speech on the ruling class. The life practices of the ruling class have reduced speech to the dictates of the practical mind and the templates of work practices. They have increased the number of expressions people refrain from saying thanks to the rules of etiquette of petty-bourgeois culture, which are embedded in business practices and spread like saliva into every cell of life. They have introduced a speech order that has become a set of expression rules. Speech practices in postmodern periods are either governed and reproduced by these templates or, in reaction to them, they take the form of a subcultural language based on violence and sexual practices. In the meaning-making processes between the templates and the response, the production of expressions far from in-depth analysis continues among individuals under the "consume fast" principle brought about by the postmodern lifestyle.

Karl Jaspers' statements in his book *Philosophical Faith* show us that the blows to the ability to analyze carry with them a different danger:

> We live in a consciousness of dangers unrecognized in past centuries: Social communication, measured in millennia, may break down, we may lose transmissions without realizing it, consciousness may diminish, the publicity of the context of what is reported may be removed. (Jaspers, 2003, p. 9).

Jaspers' resistance to this point is one of the essential characteristics of his philosophy. However, the fact that he is far from materialism and can overcome this process by escaping to the concept he expresses as transcendence is impossible. Because capitalism directly attacks the perception of time, which is necessary for philosophizing, it also attacks one of the essential transmissions Jaspers refers to. The perception of time is relative and has already begun to change since humanity dominated the night with the electric lamp. Light affects the perception of time. The primary determinant of time throughout history has been daylight. The perception of time and the vocabulary necessary to philosophize are becoming increasingly chaotic.

Basil Bernstein's theory of the relationship and difference between the "voice" and the "message" and of the limited and functional linguistic forms produced, legitimized, and reproduced by classes in society has important implications for the language practices of the working classes. Bernstein proposes two codes: restricted and elaborated. Within the restricted code, found mainly among working-class speakers, language is context-dependent and concrete and contributes to communal solidarity. Most middle-class speakers of elaborated codes maintain their roles, and their language is universalizing, abstract, formally complex, and self-reflexive. Can apply the term of this opposition to the difference between popular and high culture. According to Bernstein, working-class children's access to elaborate codes and, therefore, to the dominant culture within such regulations is also limited. This is at least cultural, perhaps cognitive, and linguistic poverty (Bernstein, 1999, p. 381). When Bernstein's ideas are considered, it is seen that elements of popular culture lead to a shaping of thought.

Another assumption on the limitation of thought by power through language is Orwell's (1999) theory. George Orwell's famous expression "Newspeak" is based on the assumption that limiting speech and language through oppression also blunts thought. Orwell exemplified this idea in his famous novel "1984." The novel's protagonist, Winston, works as an officer of a party that ensures that news reaches the public and fulfills a task related to reorganizing language. In the novel, during Winston's dialogue with Syme, a party official, Syme's words show the actualization of Newspeak:

> Destroying words is a perfect thing. Of course, predicates and adjectives are the main casualties, but hundreds of nouns need to go. It is not just synonyms, there are also antonyms. What good is a word that is the opposite of another word? Every word already carries its opposite in itself. For example, why do we need the word 'bad' when we have the word 'good'? 'Not good works better. Because it is the exact opposite of the first word, and the other is not. Alternatively, for example, a word stronger than 'good'; we do not need all these nonsense words like wonderful, marvelous, and so on, but 'plus good' gives the same meaning, or 'double plus good,' if we want a stronger word. We already use these words, but when the Yenikonush takes its final form, the

concepts of good and evil will be expressed in only six words, in fact, in a single word. (Orwell, 1999, p. 48).

Newspeak is the spoken language that the novel tries to create. Reducing the other adjectives between good and evil to six words means narrowing moral patterns, sharpening the activity of characterizing phenomena, and limiting the ability to think. The aim is to eliminate the crime of thought.

In Orwell's novel, the ruling classes control speech through institutionalized means. However, in today's societies, the structure realizes this without needing any control. Thanks to mass media and social media, the line between the public and private spheres has been thinning daily in the twentieth century. These tools, which define the "individual" and can determine many aspects of daily conversations, have marginalized political speech by relegating it to a secondary position. In the speech practices they produce in all kinds of relationships (jokes, satires, etc.), subjects communicate with templates, words, or sentences taken from TV series or movies rather than their imagination and thus think less and less. People's imaginations have been emasculated, and they consume the expressions they like from TV series or popular movies, in a sense, the templates they have bought, just like choosing goods from a shopping aisle. After finishing them for a while, they replace them with new expressions they grab from television or commercial movies. In this way, hundreds of thousands of people who have not found their selves can consume many selves through TV series or movie heroes and get rid of their absence through instant catharsis by using their expressions.

Thus, by assuming a decisive role in interpersonal communication, the mass media circulate among the masses a formation that does not contain politics and does not appear political on the surface but is, in fact, highly ideological. The control of the spoken word, which is also the determinant of collective thought, pushes politics and even philosophy out of life practices and develops the processes of "living the moment without awareness," which is the basis of the functioning of power and turns individuals into fish with three seconds of memory.

According to Negt and Kluge, all forms of bourgeois publicness are based on speaking and mimetic. A speech economy is created by emphasizing linguistic correctness and establishing a standard and single expression form. Most of this 'economic speech' is transmitted through schools and television, and these forms of speech create barriers to the communication practices of the working class (Köker, 2007, p. 115).

Emil Michel Cioran, a twentieth-century philosopher of Romanian origin who wrote in French, saw that speech had been eviscerated. In his work *The Book of Decay*, he addressed this point as follows:

Humanity would have to stop speaking to refresh language: It would use signs or, more effectively, silence. The prostitution of words is the most visible sign of its degradation; there is no longer an untouched word, no longer a pure utterance; everything loses its value repeatedly, even the things that make sense. (Cioran, 2012, p. 147).

It is necessary to analyze the evolution of the structure of speech in society and the transformation of power. Michel Foucault differs from Marxist theories about transforming the construction of power and the system of power. According to Marxist theory, power is an external element. It has apparatuses and realizes the transformation of the subject through these apparatuses. According to Foucault's theory of biopower, this transformation is realized through internal and external mechanisms. However, the fact that the thoughts of the ruling class throughout history, as Karl Marx states in "The German Ideology," are the dominant thoughts of society cannot be abstracted from the fact that power functions through internal mechanisms and does not reverse this situation. Marx summarizes this situation in his work *The German Ideology* as follows:

The thoughts of the ruling class are, in all ages, the ruling thoughts; in other words, the class which is the ruling material power of society is also the ruling mental power. The class that possesses the means of material production also possesses the means of mental production. These are so intertwined that the thoughts of those not given the means of production depend on this ruling class. Sovereign ideas are nothing but the intellectual expression of sovereign material relations, and sovereign ideas are material, sovereign relations conceived in the form of ideas; they are, therefore, the expression of the relations that make a class sovereign; in other words, they are the ideas of its sovereignty. The individuals who constitute the ruling class possess, among other things, consciousness and consequently think; as long as these individuals as a class dominate and determine the historical epoch in all its breadth, they are, of course, rulers in all the breadth of their class. They are rulers as thinkers, as producers of ideas, as well as in other things, and they regulate the production and distribution of the ideas of their epoch; their ideas are, therefore, the ruling ideas of their epoch. (Marx, 2004a, p. 75).

However, the thoughts of the ruling class dominate have changed, commodity inflation has occurred, the power of any class to control it has almost disappeared, and the process of transforming the relationship between humans and commodities has accelerated. This situation has depoliticized the word, which is inseparable from reality, day by day, turning it into a means of escape that keeps individuals away from their existential problems and the processes of holding on to the system. In its structural transformation, power supports this domesticated speech at every point for all classes. Unlike its past models, it reduces the severity of the pressures on speech. It is necessary to look at Michel Foucault's concept of power.

Foucault (2003) asserts that power derives from the relations within the spheres in which it exists. "By power, he does not mean power as a set of institutions and apparatuses that guarantee citizens' dependence within a given state. Nor is it a system of sovereignty exercised by one element or group over another group and whose effects pass through the entire social structure through successive derivations," Foucault's understanding of power. The analysis based on the concept of power deals with something other than the state's sovereignty, the form of law, or the total unity of freedom as the first data. According to Foucault, these are, instead, the ultimate forms of power. Accordingly, one must first understand the power in terms of the diversity of power relations inherent to the field in which they are exercised and that constitute their organization; that is, the movement that transforms, strengthens, and reverses these relations through struggles and confrontations. It is necessary to understand the bases that these power relations find in each other in such a way as to form a chain or a system, or on the contrary, differences and antagonisms that isolate them from each other; finally, it is necessary to understand their strategies, the general line or institutional transparency of which develops in the state apparatus, in the formulation of law and social hegemony. The volatile base of power relations brings into play situations of power with their inequalities, but always local and unstable conditions of power. It is omnipresent because it is reproduced in every moment, point, and relation between one point and another. Power is everywhere, not because it encompasses everything, but because it comes from everywhere.

One of the most critical points about discourse in Foucault's work is the dichotomy that every discourse has. Dichotomies are opposition structures inherent in lessons: Bright vs. crazy, moral vs. vagabond, hardworking vs. lazy, rich vs. poor, harmonious vs. disharmonious, heterosexual vs. homosexual, etc. Power is concentrated on one side of these dichotomies, and the dichotomies that infiltrate discourses also construct the mind. A system that looks positive evokes the positive and, therefore, produces and feeds on choices, values, judgments, and even desires, which are established through the performativity of these discourses.

According to Marxist theories, power has a series of practices that spread from top to bottom, whereas in Foucault, this is not the case. Power is distributed to every point and every element that constitutes society. In this context, the signs and speech circulating in the community are the agents of influence. The expansion of visual culture and the transformation of society into a virtual planet of icons transform and limit thinking and, thus, speech. Where Foucault differs in functioning and agency - for Foucault, power is passive - it unites with Marxist theories in transforming the subject. The fact that speech is an instrument of power should be evaluated precisely within Foucault's theory of power.

The pre-modern subject reads beyond the signified according to a specific paradigm and dogma based on the aprioristic judgments it accepts, following the laziness of human nature without thinking about it. Since the subject of modern and post-modern society has lost the ready-made road maps through which it can reach the signified, it goes through a rapid consumption in the pool of signifiers and strives to form new combinations of signifiers to fill the anguish of haplessness and immobility that it suffers due to the "death of God." The more he tries, the more he gets bogged down in the quagmire of meaning. The value given to fast-flowing signifiers and the new type of commodity fetishism reflects the longing for the maps of sense that their ancestors had. The result is either nostalgia or wandering like "sheep on the small mounds of pleasure of the moment." The massive erosion of the signifier-signified relationship has led to the grotesque destruction of all life practices, primarily speech/parole.

In a world where everything has turned upside down, keeping silent from now on is the true face of resistance!

The commodity is, in a way, anarchist in terms of the debate it carries within it. In the Foucauldian sense, it erodes the power produced everywhere and infiltrates everywhere. Making a new one in its place degenerates the existing one in a structure as micro as Heraclitus's statement, "You cannot enter the same river twice." In every period of history, it attacks the dominant ideas of the period in which it exists from the front with an acceleration depending on the speed of the trade cycle and technological developments in the means of production, wears them down, and sows the seeds of the paradigm it will establish.

Language, on the other hand, is conservative. It takes a long time to change, is anonymous, and is directly linked to generations. It establishes the dominant paradigm and socializes people accordingly. Being a lazy animal is human by nature; the ability to break the structure depends on traumas and luck. Due to the interaction of the primary institutions of the system with human beings, language still reflects both sides of the dialectic.

As Karl Marx put it, history is the history of class wars. However, a break occurred when speech was detached from the subject and could be transmitted. From then on, the cultural history of societies is the history of the war between language and commodity. The anarchist structure of the item versus the conservatism of language is in conflict everywhere. Moreover, the thing, stripped of its guerrilla tactics after the Industrial Revolution, has been openly attacking speech for the last two hundred years. The commodity inflation and the rapid evolution of the commodity from the concrete to the abstract are attacking the dominant paradigm and its most vigorous defenders, language, so hard that the structural institutions of language are collapsing at an unprecedented rate. A capitalist hegemony has resulted in languages of cultures that have made inroads into capitalism, flooding the languages of peoples of the Third World. At the same time, most objects that subjects see around them remain nameless in their consciousness and are referred to as "things."

Sensing this situation, Baudrillard states that in the 1960s, production lost its privileged position, and a new social regime emerged. The society of consumption became more prominent than the society of production. He says the semiotic system formed by the objects produced establishes a new syntactic relationship between them. According to the thinker, the object has started to live in a universe where the signifier overrides the "thing" it shows, hides it, and nothing is as it seems (Baudrillard, 2005, p. 18).

During this time, the commodity has taken over the greatest weapon of language, the word, and has become able to produce it under its sovereignty. The term is no longer the weapon of language but of the commodity. Whereas in societies not invaded by things, the commercial product produced, in other words, the item, depending on the structure formed by language, today, the main force that constitutes power in the Foucauldian sense is no longer just language. We are in an atmosphere where the word barely catches up with what is produced when the produced commodity is adapted to the language. Had the term based on the dominant language in this relationship? In addition to gaining meaning through its relationship with other items beyond the structure of language while being co-located, it crosses language in a transcendent manner. In such an atmosphere, language is lost in the duel for the word. Since the produced commodity does not need to sit somewhere in the language, the term "thing" dominates the speech and is perhaps the most used word. Too many "things" can now be described with too few words. "Thing" is the speech key of the postmodern world. Confirming Frederich Jameson's statement that "the truth of experience no longer coincides with the place in which it occurs," countless signs merge with the signifier "thing" before they can be experienced.

Compared to previous generations, the postmodern consumer is genuinely ignorant about the production processes through which their consumption is produced. No era in history is as innocent about what it's consumed as today's people. The postmodern consumer, who is completely detached from craft knowledge, who does not know how to sew clothes, who does not learn how bread is processed, calls everything a "thing" in the world of false hedonism created by commodities and operates the wheels of the capitalist system while demanding a new one and a newer one.

"Thing," perhaps the most used word of the new generations born into a symbolic hedonism, has become the keyword of millions of people who form their images in bundles of messages much more than previous generations, who are equipped with symbols created by very new institutions other than natural ways and a natural speed. This word becomes a code that swallows up millions of meanings in one fell swoop as if identified with everything that attacks humanity and merges with all kinds of power processes in everyday language. The "thing" floods the social consciousness by combining with phenomena that make human beings human, such as individual isolation, the emasculation of the ability to make sense, the day-by-day decrease in the ability to question, and the sterilization of intellectual tools in proportion to the reduction in the number of words used. The attack, symbolized by this word, has reached a dimension that endangers humanity as the power produced by the capitalist economy has attained the apparatuses of biopower with which it can create subjects. The modern consumer economy owes its existence precisely to the tendency of issues to pursue pleasure and gratification. While fun and enjoyment were mainly derived from the use value of the commodity in pre-industrial revolution societies, in industrial organization, the exchange value came to the fore. Postmodern culture has turned this exchange value into a process of extremes in addition to focusing on consuming symbols. The basis of symbolic hedonism is the subject's escape from the world. Imagination machines, each of which is the black holes of the "Virtual Icon Planet," realize the subject's connection with the natural world and recognize the issue's existence through symbolic consumption while simultaneously imprisoning it on a ground covered with objects. Every age creates its own needs, and human needs are not universal except for basic biological needs. Billions of people who have become the laughingstock of a global game legitimize this situation in all kinds of consumption rituals. Turning every disappointment in their lives into greed and want, this vast herd of idiots attacks the shopping centers and their postmodern sanctuaries like locusts during every kind of leisure time (holidays, New Year's, weekends, etc.) organized to satisfy their new needs produced by the system.

Between 1983 and 1987, 51 million microwave ovens, 44 million washing machines and dryers, 85 million color televisions, 36 million refrigerators and coolers, 48 million videocassette recorders, and 23 million cordless telephones were sold in the United States, with an adult population of only 180 million (Schor, 1991, p. 108). All these products, while reaching their buyers worldwide, not only spread their intended use to the world but also supported the establishment of a holistic lifestyle. With the rise of individualism after Fordist production in the 1970s, concepts such as mass production, mass communication, mass transportation, propaganda for the masses, etc., created by the Fordist economy and contradicted individualism, came to an end. The postmodern era isolates the individual and does not even see them in a mass. The economy, which is moving towards a production technology that can produce according to the subject's preference and is so advanced that it can almost make for each individual, is about to create the isolated issue, in other words, the "individual," which was a nineteenth-century delusion. This individual is a new person, equipped with the delusion that it is detached from and independent of society, positioned as the dictator of its own world, and can use very few words. The late eighteenth-century American and French Revolutions aimed at this project, but the postmodern era is successfully building it. Except for the postmodern period, individualism has never been so practiced and expanded to include all classes. The recent development of biopower tools is the main factor in this expansion. According to Revel (2006, p. 119), the concept of the individual is itself a political creation. The idea of the individual is not identical to the image of the person: It came into being in the seventeenth century, when the concept of the citizen in the modern sense emerged, that is, in a context based on the contract (social contract). The idea of the individual has its roots in the secular construction of the citizen, which became evident with the formation of modern nation-states. The individual is not the expression of a singularity that stands in opposition to all non-specific mass appearances – the mass, the people, the class, the party – but rather what is produced by the same logical structure of the world, what is part of the same political grammar: It belongs to the current configuration of power.

At the end of the twentieth century, time control spread worldwide, and punctuality became a universal concept; subjects' lives were compartmentalized in addition to their daily lives, such as their working hours, overtime, retirement, etc. The events that transform their perceptions of time, as well as their perception of space, are the imagination machines. The passive control of their perception of time and distance directly controls their lives, and this naturally affects their speech practices.

The metropolis is the focal point of the culture of commodification in capitalism, where everything is commodified, including time. Almost all idealized life forms of the system are also found in the metropolis. While the language of the municipality dominates the language of the media, the majority of the lifestyles presented in the means of communication are metropolitan lifestyles. The main criterion in all bio-political productions/productions of subjectivity is urban qualities, sometimes actively and sometimes passively. As Antonio Negri puts it, as soon as the production of capital overflows from factory spaces, it turns the whole society into an area of production spaces. It transforms the entire community into an organic mechanism in terms of production and production of subjectivity. Qualities traditionally associated with the metropolis, such as communication, unexpected encounters with social difference, access to the common, and the production of collective forms of life, increasingly characterize both urban and rural environments today and are central elements in biopolitical production. Social life produces and is produced in this metropolitan space (Hardt and Negri, 2011a, p. 245).

Especially after the Second World War, when television became widespread, all forms of communication between people have come under the direct influence of the media and indirectly of corporations. Many products of the culture industry, from advertisements to television series, have reached a power that determines not only what people will talk about but also what they will talk about, in what manner, and how they will talk about it. The way people speak, the clothes they wear, and the words that have become popular all resemble those of television stars, and they make sense of life through the frames they draw. Their relationships are no different from those in movies and TV series, and they are forced to consume energy without direction, angle, or perspective. Advertisements have already placed children in their target audience, and advertisement producers have discovered how to influence their parents. Even the conversations between children and their parents can be relatively controlled. Lucy Hughes, head of the strategy at Initiative Madia, one of the world's largest media companies, is chilling. Hughes realized that advertising should not be aimed at getting children to buy things but at getting them to nag their parents to buy something, which illustrates the nag factor. To achieve this goal, Hughes and his colleagues, with the help of child psychologists, developed a scientific analysis of the different types of nagging used by children and their effects on different types of parents (Bakan, 2007, p. 148). Recognizing the influence of children on their parents, advertisers target the subjects of the future market from an early age and direct their minds.

Where are the words in an atmosphere where images of commodities and even independent images of items are constantly circulating? Do we see the relationship between words and thought evolving into a relationship between ideas and thought? The answer to this question may be "yes." However, there is still a severe struggle. Words and pictures clash to represent thought. Images go one step further in this battle every day. One of the most significant proofs of this is. We remember the pictures of many people around us, not their names.

Similarly, another proof is that humanity's vocabulary and the number of words we use in everyday speech are steadily declining. The decline in the number of terms of daily use relative to commodity inflation means that the topics people are interested in are narrow, and the words they use to reflect can apply this word for only a few manifestations. When images were not so widespread, words often came between objects and people. Each object corresponds to a word in the mind. Today, we are witnessing the destruction of this.

Irigaray (2021) questions whether "a language is a tool that allows us to appropriate everything that surrounds us and bend it to our use" and asks whether the function of speech is to particularize the world or contribute to a transformation compatible with becoming. Does speech function in such a way that instead of sprouting the human being, it detaches them more from life?

The commercialization of speech accelerates its transformation into a state that detaches human beings from whatever source or essence they have. With commercialized speech has come an age in which the potential of speech to support human existence and increase the possibilities of human self-realization is diminishing by the day. Instead of enabling and enabling the person to dwell in themselves, commercialized speech distorts the person from themselves and exiles them to themselves. The commercialization of speech has moved the conversation between two people or a group into another sphere, disrupting mutual learning and development possibilities, which is now considered "normal."

Suppose those who made money from rhetoric lessons and letters in ancient Greece do not count as the beginning of this alienation. This commercialization can be traced back to the massification of telephones and radios. The ability to simultaneously transmit speech to a distant place is linked to the history of technological developments and massification.

Electromagnetic transmission was successfully applied to speech transmission in the 1870s and formed the basis for developing commercially available telephone systems. In the last decade of the nineteenth century, Tesla, Marconi, and others began to address the problem of the need for transmission wires through their experiments in the transmission of signals employing electronic waves. Fessenden and others developed the technology of speech transmission using electronic waves in the first decade of the twentieth century (Thompson, 2008, p. 126).

The history of telephones began in 1876 with the work of Alexander Graham Bell (1847–1922), an American of Scottish descent. "Telephone," the name of the device he patented, was first used in 1796 for an acoustic method of communication. From the start, Bell proved to himself that he was more than an inventor. After he visited England, he set up what was called a "great system." He realized what may sound utopian: "a universal network to homes, offices, and businesses – built numerous switchboards for this purpose. In 1878, New Heaven installed the first switchboard, and in 1879, Coleman Street opened the first telephone office in London. It would be long before the telephone became an ordinary household appliance" (Briggs and Burke, 2021, p. 168).

When Alexander Graham Bell made the first telephone, he was trying to develop the telegraph further. In mid-1876, the telephone business was still in its infancy. About 10,000 Bell devices were used nationwide, but now Bell faces severe competition. Western Union, which had set up telegraph offices almost everywhere, began to offer a competing service using telephones designed by Thomas Edison and Elisha Gray (Crowley and Heyer, 2017, p. 219).

In the 1880s, a typical telephone system was cumbersome. Three boxes made up the device. A magneto generator, a lever, and a bell were in the top box. The middle box contained a speaking tube to be brought forward and a listening tube suspended from the side. The third box contained a liquid battery that had to be refilled at intervals and occasionally leaked. The caller turned the handle to alert the switchboard operator; the alert signal caused a cover on the central office switch panel to open mechanically, revealing the location of the call. The operator inserted the headset into the slot and asked the caller. The operator then rang the ringer for the called party and connected them using cables and sockets on the switch panel. The two parties spoke, usually loudly and clearly, and hung up (Crowley and Heyer, 2017, p. 220).

Who were the first telephone subscribers? Among the first users, professionals who urgently needed to reach people started to use the telephone first. Doctors were, therefore, prominent. The phone was helpful because it allowed them to be quickly informed about emergencies and to make appointments when not in their offices. Often, pharmacists also had telephones. But the primary market was for the wealthy. Over time, it became clear that some businessmen were reluctant to use telephones rather than telegraphs because they valued the written record more.

Nevertheless, some manufacturers, lawyers, bankers, and small shopkeepers embraced the technology. Telephone technology, which spread rapidly in the early years, could not extend to the general public due to monopoly prices. People continued to use the telegraph and postal services for some time.

In 1900, mass journalism depended more on the telephone than telegraph communication in the USA. Until 1922, Paris was cautious about using the phone, which remained a tool for professional people only. In 1900, the United States was far ahead of all European countries regarding telephone distribution. There was one telephone for every sixty people. Sweden, with one telephone for every 215 people, took first place among European countries (Briggs and Burke, 2021, p. 171).

The detachment of the spatialization of the spoken word and the mass media has brought along a series of effects that make it independent from time-space. By detaching from time and space, the articulated word experiences time-space dissociation. According to Thompson (2008), in the case of face-to-face conversation, time-space dissociation is relatively tiny. Dialogue takes place in the context of communal co-presence. The participants in the discussion are physically in the same place, sharing similar temporal-spatial sets of referents (very similar sets). The utterances exchanged in speech are usually addressed only to those engaged in the mutual activity or to individuals nearby. The statements cannot go beyond the moments of transition or fading memory during their exchange (Thompson, 2008, p. 43). By eliminating this, the mass media give the spoken word the advantage of being recorded and, simultaneously, break its connection with space. However, it transforms the casual relationship of face-to-face communication into a monologue. The medium creates large masses of listeners and directs one's consciousness. The messages received control people's way of life and their ability to speak and, therefore, to think.

People actively shape the self through the meaningful content and messaging media products provide. This process is not sudden, one-off, and for all events. It unfolds gradually, imperceptibly, day by day, year by year. Some messages we retain, some we forget, and some we act upon, reflect upon, or discuss among friends. Others slip out of a person's memory, lost in a constant stream of images and ideas (Thompson, 2008, p. 74).

According to Volaşinov, the concept of consciousness is material and is formed by interpreting external signs by signs within consciousness. Signs emerge only in the interaction process between one individual consciousness and another. Individual consciousness itself is full of signs. Consciousness becomes consciousness only after it is filled with ideological (signifying) content and, consequently, only in social interaction (Volaşinov, 2001, p. 51). In this sense, the communication apparatus influences mass consciousness is transformation. As McLuhan (2001) emphasizes, "The medium is the message". The telephone is one of the tools that intensify this interaction.

Martin Cooper was an engineer at Motorola. Born into an immigrant family and a submarine officer in the Korean War may have contributed to the technology that led to the cell phone. Working on this topic in the 1960s, Cooper invented the radio, the ancestor of the cell phone. In 1973, Motorola launched a product that liberated the phone from being tied to a cable. Like almost every other invention, the cell phone, which first entered the service of the military and then the capitalists as a class, initially weighed about 1 kg.

Telephone conversations were initially a format with limited communication qualities. It was a communication style with less symbolic solid interaction than face-to-face interaction. Today, however, new cell phone technologies can transmit many more messages. Participants, of course, still need to be in the exact spatial location. However, thanks to video telephony, the area of the speakers is mutually known. Temporally, the telephone is a means of communication in which both parties share an expected time, something that changes with voice recorders. However, due to its nature, the medium needed to be more suitable for long conversations in the past. It was a fast and direct communication tool for a specific purpose. Today, however, the cell phone has become a tool aimed at the person's psychology without the purpose of the action. The reason for using the cell phone has turned into the fear of loneliness behind the veil of reaching other people and the need for confidence that one is in society.

Thanks to post Fordist production technologies, the cell phone, like other commodities in society, has diversified and become a status indicator. These devices, whose features and prices change accordingly, confer status to their owners in terms of brand value. Today, quality is determined by the commodities one owns rather than the social groups one belongs to or class characteristics.

In early 2000, four major mobile phone companies in the UK were Vodafone, BT Cellnet, One2One, and Orange, the last of which quickly acquired 1.2 million customers between April and June 2000. A total of 7.2 million users will then be reached. The global market is still not saturated, and numerous national and international initiatives are being undertaken (Briggs and Burke, 2021, p. 329).

And what about the excessive attention that post-industrial companies pay to cell phones? Due to cell phones, these companies are eliminating the distinction between personal and professional lives. In the UK, zero-hour, not part-time, employment contracts are drawn up and accompanied by a cell phone. When the company needs you, they pick up the phone, and you run to work! Domestic slavery is being reinvented here. The electronic detention to which criminals are subjected in the closed circuit of a police station is also a phenomenon of this kind (Virilio, 2021, p. 67).

Image support also allows complete control of speech's content within the image's power. In the preface to his monumental work *Phanomenologe des Geistes* (*Phanomenologe des Geistes*), written in 1807, Hegel writes that the fullness and seriousness of life are spiritually present in the experience and that this is reflected, appropriately enough, in everyday speech. It is precisely a loss of spirit that occurs when image and speech merge. Speech is now detached from experience and dominated by the image.

Thanks to technology, the human mouth and the act of speaking have become detached from space and time. Various tools have separated speech from the area and spread it across the globe, from telephones to radios to televisions to the internet. On the other hand, recording devices protect it against time and make it preservable. As such, we can easily claim that "Never in any age has discourse been produced to this extent." The increase in the world population compared to previous times also supports this argument. However, the point to be emphasized here reveals whose discourses are dominant. Capital owners have the means to direct the discourses of societies.

The radio, invented in 1895, 15 years after the invention of the telephone, was, like other technological devices, the result of a series of inventions. However, five names stand out in the invention of the radio: Popov, Hertz, Maxwell, Tesla, and Marconi. Communication Workers' Day, as it is known in Russia, and Radio and Television Day, officially known in Bulgaria, commemorate the invention of the radio in Russia. Radio Day is celebrated every year in that region on May 7th. This day was chosen because Alexander Stepanovich Popov successfully demonstrated the radio he invented on May 7th, 1895. Popov publicly demonstrated his invention in St. Petersburg, Russia, and is recognized as the inventor of the radio in Eastern Europe. However, in the West, Marconi is known as the inventor of the radio. The radio, whose first use was in the shipping field, rapidly became widespread, including overseas communication, when it was proved in 1923 that high-frequency radio waves hit the ionosphere and returned to Earth. It is one of the most effective tools in the history of communication, with its propaganda power and functionality in the Second World War.

Since radio was the first mass communication tool and the first means of bringing regulated discourse into people's most private spheres, it significantly affected the dissemination of the dominant discourse. It is challenging to imagine this in today's eye-centered communication tools. There is a compelling speech that can speak in people's lives, in their most intimate spaces, the living rooms of their homes, and is listened to as the discourse of power. The radio has replaced the "father's speech", who is considered the house expert. The state is now the birth "father of the family" regarding the trust and power of discourse. There are now two head figures in the house: the state and the head of the family. The information depends on the organization of life, the subject, and even communication between people. The radio speaks as the family's expert. The radio is an authority of its time. People listen to it, and they cannot answer it. As McLuhan says, the medium has become the message itself. The medium is power; just like the dictatorial world of its time, it is authoritarian. From Hitler to Stalin, Salazar to Mustafa Kemal, and Petain to Hideko Tojo, when there were dictators worldwide, radio was the voice of all of them.

Radio is a foreign discourse entering the household. It is the first medium that brings the speech of many personalities outside the home into the home. Lessons begin with the press of a button. Therefore, the first radios are state monopolies. The control and nationalization of foreign discourse in the house is the fundamental basis for the nation-state here. This medium, which carries speeches outside the home to the home, has become a home member. From now on, people will get used to living together not only with the discourses in their households, villages, neighborhoods, and streets but also with the voice of the state, which they see as a potent authority. Radio is the beginning of this.

Initially, the language on the radio was strictly the national language. National languages are the common language of the ruling classes, whose interests are exploited by the masses, and radio discourses are the discourse of the ruling classes. The situation in the colonies is similar to that of the nation-states. The state language on the radio is the language of the colonizer. Therefore, common representations such as homeland, flag, national anthem, state, soldier, etc., are the most prominent messages of the first radios. A foreign language other than the ordinary and determined language cannot exist on the radio. A foreign language is the other and is an enemy or an agent. Thanks to radio, the cohesiveness of language in culture has become much more robust.

In his work *On Hospitality*, Derrida states: "Language resists all transformations because it moves with me. Language is the most irreplaceable thing" (2020, p. 81). Derrida, who says that Language is the most resistant of the fantasies within the established structure, refers to the counter-revolutionary quality mentioned here. Language is the glue of the system. A glue that prevents all known elements from flying in the atmosphere of meaning.

Language is also the source of marginalization. The "other" with whom one does not share the same language or cannot meet on the exact text is the other. The language referred to here is speech and the language that covers all kinds of texts. The text of clothing, the text of gender, the text of nutrition, etc. All the texts that make up the structure appear normal to humans, and going outside the language of these texts leads to being labeled as "other." The minds produced through language ensure this, and it is precisely at this point that language acts as a glue. It holds mental structures together.

The circulation of what is produced in the market determines the circulation of the word. Long before the current trade cycle, words were influenced by the cycle of market relations, even for the barter trade systems of early human societies. Barter or barter is a trade-in in which goods are exchanged for each other rather than for money.

Since the tribes spoke different languages, people had to resort to sign language during the exchange. When they returned to their tribes, they brought things and foreign words they had adopted without realizing it. Thus, the tribes' languages, comments, and ideas were mixed (Ilin and Segal, 2016, p. 65). As this trade accelerated, so did the circulation of words; today, this speed is relatively high. Although nation-states try to barricade this acceleration with various institutions and language protection laws, this is futile in the face of the realities of the historical relationship between the word and the commodity. Words spread with the spread of products, and the languages of the centers that dominate the production-consumption relationship will dominate in the regions where markets are concentrated. This market is now the whole world.

Byung-Chul Han expands on Heidegger's concept of "pure closeness that endures distance" and says that this negativity must be eliminated in a suffering society (2022, p. 29). The "society of transparency" that Han refers to (2022), in which negativity and pain are tried to be eliminated, is a society in which visibility destroys meaning. Heidegger speaks of a "pure closeness that endures distance." One can no longer say of closeness. In proximity, there is still separation and separateness. In this new society, there is no void. Everything is compressed like a "Zip file." In this way, complexity overcomes meaning and destroys it. Meaning wastes time and slows down. Dealing with sense is a waste of energy. At such speed, every action is the enemy of meaning, and everything is a meaningless image. The system has become total pornocracy. It's nothing more than a pornocracy. There are very few Democrats anymore. The masses who worship images and lack meaning can only be pornocrats. Democracy is dead in an environment where fitness trumps meaning. In a world where cosmetics shops outnumber and are valued far more than bookstores, pornocrats will outnumber Democrats.

The tenth-century period known as the *Saeculum Obscurum*, the height of papal depravity, is described as a reasonable period of disambiguation. Beginning in the 920s, the incredible events that took place under the rule of the Hariots are considered the most terrible period in Christianity and lasted for 60 years. The Theophylacti were an aristocratic family that ruled for two hundred years, and the popes brought all kinds of immorality to their peak (Dwyer, 1998). Since Theophylact, his wife Theodora, and daughter Marozia's concubinage relations with the popes and their exploitation of the subjects were legendary, German theologians in the nineteenth century called the period "pornocracy" in their works (Squatriti, 2014).

This short period of 60 years took place in a small geographical area. The second period of pornocracy has now spread all over the world. Pornocracy is the height of image society. There is no longer a language in the classical sense. In parallel with the history of colonialism, there is a situation beyond the dominance of English. English is a deep language like any other language, but no Shakespeare exists. There is a package language derived from English and adapted to the speed of social media. There is a "packaged language" that is low in words, detached from grammar, unable to convey more than a shallow thought, and includes emojis in its alphabet. This packaged language is the language of pornocracy.

In a pornocratic society, people don't have different ideologies. Everyone is a pornocrat. A pornocrat is a collage of many ideologies and advocates a nation-state but at the same time winks at international ideas. On the one hand, it is an animal lover, but on the other hand, it consumes animal products. A pornocrat takes sides in conflicts between states, often in favor of his nation-state, but at the same time, it may have a moral anti-war sentiment. They may support the guerrillas seeking independence but be insensitive to the people exploited by their state within the borders of their own country when a state exploits people far away from their country. Because they do not know ideologies profoundly, and even if they do, they cannot internalize them.

Communication cannot lighten the burden of the soul if it does not carry a ritual context of meaning. *Ayin* means tradition in Turkish. *Töre*, on the other hand, gives confidence because it is known and carried through generations. A ritual does not harm society for an extended period. As a result of changing material conditions, of course, some rituals are harmful. However, each carried operational burdens at a specific time in the past. Therefore, in the collective unconscious, these burdens leave sediments due to being carried for a long time. In pornocracies, communication is detached from ritual. Ritualized communication elements do not reduce the burden but add to it. This break with ritual brings with it excessive questioning of the message. Even though people constantly talk to each other through various means, they cannot empty and relax because they have become detached from the ritual elements of communication. Talking is no longer a release; it is a state of burden.

Sahlins (2019, p. 17) describes a period similar to that in Thucydides' account of a civil war in Corfu during the Peloponnesian War in the fifth century BC. During this civil war, self-interest became such that Thucydides comments that "even words changed their meanings and now had to take on new meanings given to them." Thucydides refers to the situation we see today in many languages where words can be used interchangeably for morally contradictory situations. This is a sign of crisis, but even the most brutal rules are becoming the "norm."

Moreover, this norm universalizes speech and attitudes in a world where the image has spread and become more central to life than ever before. Television and cinema became widespread worldwide after the Second World War, and social media through the internet have turned the world into a giant screen.

In a world where attitudes are universalized, how much can we talk about locality anymore? At no point in history have the subjects' attitudes been as rational as modernity would like them to be. Forms of rational behavior have been produced and taken on an international character. However, humans are not suitable for the sheath of rationality that modernity demands. The rational human being is a modern myth. The human being, who has acted intensely with conditioned reflexes in every period, has turned into an absolute idiot in today's world. Wrapped up in automatic thoughts, humans wander on the verge of being unable to decide right and wrong since most of the external messages that make up the consciousness are virtual. According to Virilio, the massification of attitudes, also statistically determined today, threatens democracy (Virilio, 2021, p. 65).

If humanity had to vote today on a model of the world and a way of life, it would undoubtedly succeed. In the meantime, more than 500 satellites are actively working, scanning the Earth with their advanced signals. The same yearning of people living around the Amur, Jangtse, Amazon, Ganges, and Nile rivers is fed by uniform images on billions of television screens. Satellite dishes and solar collectors transport millions of people from their villages to planetary dimensions, even in remote areas such as Nigeria in western Africa (Martin and Schumann, 2007, p. 25). In such an environment, one cannot speak of a local perception, nor can one speak of a local human attitude. As the local is transformed day by day at the speed of melting ice in the middle of the desert, even the forms of speech that have become the common fantasy of existence are becoming universal, albeit in different languages.

As with massifying attitudes, areas of interest, reactions to phenomena, and language are becoming uniform. As appearance, image, and style become increasingly essential building blocks of social identities, media images direct how individuals perceive people and shape how people are publicly evaluated and defined (Kellner, 2020, p. 217). The opposition of subjects is regulated, and even dissent is shaped in the way the system wants. Television is a very effective mass media at this point. The presentation of reactions against the government needs to be more diverse. Opposition within the framework of anarchist or communist ideas is not presented on television. Thus, the system is presented as if it has no alternative, as if it stems from human nature.

The divisive nature of television on perception stems from its editing. Repeatedly interrupting programs with commercials undermines our ability to perceive phenomena holistically. The information received from television is weak and insufficient in terms of content. However, those stretched between their perceptions and reality by television consider the information they receive from the medium interrupted by advertisements as sufficient. According to Schiller, in addition to its well-known functions of accelerating sales, whipping up the desire to consume, creating new needs, and facilitating the functioning of the current order, advertisements provide another unique service to the capitalist economy. Adding all kinds of news to the flow of information deepens the citizenry's incapacity to comprehend it all. As a result, it becomes easier to conceal the truth (Schiller, 2022, p. 42).

The shattering of perception by the flow of images on social media is even more terrifying than television. At every age, people have, to a certain extent, been disconnected from the alphabetical system and reading. Today, however, even the minds of those who read are succumbing to the atmosphere of the society of the spectacle. Even the alphabetic codes entered through reading and writing are doomed to drown in the vast ocean of images and pictures. The signifier has become detached from its signified, and the signified has turned into a simulacrum, as Baudrillard (2016) emphasizes.

Thanks to its unique logic, the spectacle has become widespread in all forms of culture and many new areas of social life. With their high-tech special effects, movies have become ever more spectacular and dazzling, expanding the scope of the cinematographic spectacle. Throughout the day, there is a proliferation of television channels broadcasting movies, news, political debates, sports, marketing programs, re-runs of television history, and anything else that can win them an audience (Kellner, 2020, p. 8). The spectacle is not a collection of images but a social relationship that exists between individuals and is mediated by images (Debord, 2021, p. 22)

On the other hand, Ludwig Wittgenstein stated that the formation of words occurs within people's lifestyles, that the activities during the instrumental use of language affect the meanings of words, and that linguistic activities are expressions of lifestyles. Wittgenstein stated that the meaning of each word in the vocabulary, exemplified by the "toolbox" metaphor, can gain meaning within the whole sentence and that this depends on life practices. When Witgeinstein's statements are considered, social media can completely transform human consciousness after a certain period. This transformation can bring about a whole new humanity after a short time. Speech may become a counter-revolutionary structure and a greater hegemony than ever before.

Considering that consciousness is dependent on external indicators, the extent to which the proliferation of visual culture and the sophistication of the reproducibility of photography have the power to influence human beings can be better understood. First, it is necessary to emphasize the icon inflation caused by television, the most widespread mass communication systems, and the transformation of newspapers into visual rather than written media. The icon limits the imagination and is much more potent in its ability to dictate while conveying information. It is also here that cinema derives its propaganda power. While literature allows for a much more comprehensive range of activities in terms of imagination, visual communication tools are more sterilizing at this point. From this point of view alone, the "word" that the human type dominated by visual culture disseminates will weaken and lose some signifying practices. According to Jacques Ellul, the word is also the source of a particular way of thinking. Experience tends to show that the person who thinks in images becomes less and less capable of thinking by reasoning and vice versa. The intellectual process based on images contradicts the reasoning associated with the word (Ellul, 2004, p. 271).

According to Roland Barthes, the world is overflowing with signs. Not all of these signs can be as simple as the letters of the alphabet, the signs on a transportation code, or military uniforms: There are infinitely more intricate, more complex ones. They are mostly accepted as natural knowledge (Barthes,

2005, p. 186). In this sense, the individual's consciousness is formed through a structure of signs constantly interacting with the system.

The reproducibility of nature has been recognized from the earliest periods of human self-awareness, perhaps with the first paintings drawn in the Altamira Cave. Language and art have assumed this reproductive function. However, as Roland Barthes puts it, photography is distinguished from all other signs by its ability to transform the referent into a symbol directly. As Susan Sontag (1999, p. 106) puts it, this makes it a real impostor: "Photography claims to be true in a way that paintings never can be." The social change in the years when visual culture began to emerge is perfectly summarized in Henri Lefebvre's words:

> A hundred years ago, in the social context, in the periphery of speech and discourse, concrete referents dominated. The referents, interconnected without forming a formalized system, have a unity, if not a logical coherence. There was a unity of these referents reflected in material perception (Euclidean three-dimensional space; time divided into seconds, minutes, hours), in the perception of nature, of historical recollection, of the city and its urban environment, of generally accepted ethics and aesthetics, in logic and common sense. The global character of this society as 'subject' could thus be perceived; it had (or thought it had, which is the same thing) a dominant, general code of integrity, honor, and self-respect. This society linked productive activities and creative 'values' to production. In this sense, Capital (1867) linked theoretical language to a philosophical 'consensus' that was not much known outside this work, not much known, and not much aware of its situation. 'Man' and 'humanity,' like the subject, were no longer seen as a self, an abstract essence. Human beings and humanity were defined as specific and concrete 'subjects,' acts, and agencies, affecting specific and concrete 'objects' in a historical context and directed towards 'goals.' Despite, or perhaps because of, conflicts, the praxis of this society (competitive capitalism) had a unity. (Lefebvre, 1998, p. 113-114).

The unity of praxis was shattered after the Second World War. It is the basis of social transformation that changes in science, and technology affect the means of production and the rate of change of the commodity in society. The 1960s, when Lefebvre wrote these sentences, was a period of this transformation. There is a transition from oral to written and visual culture, which has caused a significant change in human perception of time-space.

Image-based technology has an important place among the definitions of modern society. One cannot speak of a modern society where the image does not exist. According to Susan Sontag, one of its primary activities must be producing and consuming ideas for a society to be modern. Images, which have the extraordinary power to determine our claims on reality and are themselves coveted surrogates of first-hand experience, must become indispensable for the economy's health, the stability of government, and the achievement of personal happiness (Sontag, 1999, p. 171). Many objects of modern society are united in consciousness by their images and reality. It is a distinctive characteristic of the contemporary individual that their memory of the past is derived from visual means and that, despite the smallness of one's world, one is aware of a vast world – and this awareness is by no means innocent. With the invention of photography and the popularization of cinema and television, the historical consciousness of the individual socialized in visual culture has been shaped differently from the historical consciousness of people who did not have these tools. The photographic image strongly influences the construction of knowledge about the past. When one thinks of England in the 1800s, Turkey in the 1960s, or the Soviet Revolution, a surface of cinematic and photographic images, an iconic visual consciousness, is formed in mind. Within the scope of anti-communist propaganda, Soviet everyday life is gray and gloomy. Despite being surrounded by seas on three sides, many people think of Turkey as a desert. The reason for these visions is visual culture. In this context, visual culture provides control not only through its ability to popularize consumption and the fact that it is itself a commodity of consumption but also through the historical consciousness it creates. The fact that photographs claim to represent reality is a fraud by their very nature. The picture needs to be more accurate. But it makes us forget this and claims to be confirmed. It is a chemical process that presents the point of view of one of an infinite number of analytical points around the object and presents it as an image of reality. However, no other tool can be expected from an age in which the only thing sacred is an illusion, and the truth is veiled at every point. As Guy Debord puts it, in an indeed upended world, truth is a moment of falsehood (Debord, 2021, p. 38).

Many shocking examples can be cited on many issues related to the fracturing of consciousness by visual culture and, thus, its gigantic effects on speech. According to Neil Postman (1995), while in a literate world, it is affirmed that children behave like adults and have a mature attitude through disciplinary upbringing, in an illiterate world, the distinction between adult and child is not as sharp as in modern and later times. This is how the carnivalesque culture of the Middle Ages and the childlike behavior of individuals should be understood.

To be an adult in a literary world implies the possession of cultural secrets encoded in unnatural or artificial symbols. In a literate world, children must be adults. But in an illiterate world, there is no need to make a sharp distinction between child and adult because there are few secrets that children do not know in the adult world, and culture does not require training to understand it (Postman, 1995, p. 26).

Visual culture seems to be a culture that tends to return to the carnivalesque of medieval society. However, the carnivalesque culture Bakhtin (2001) speaks of requires direct and egalitarian participation. A democratic and egalitarian culture is formed through direct participation, not one in which the spectators are passively excluded. Moreover, this carnivalesque culture does not affirm culture and is not a reflection of thousands of years of accumulation but instead blesses a way of life that is directly determined by monetary policies, a way of life that oppresses the subject. The gradual decline in the importance of literacy compared to other acts of communication expands a bourgeois culture that is highly dependent on imitation and keeps even middle-aged and late-aged people stuck in adolescent behavior. The proliferation of the society of the spectacle has made an unhealthy carnival culture dominant over the entire functioning of society; the escape from the suffering arising from the nature of the political economy, which exploits people, has infiltrated the formation of all behavior patterns. Subjects now refuse to be disciplined and cannot skip the stages of being children, armed with the desire to return to childhood and to form their individuality, in other words, with the impulse to be different. Childhood and its urge to consume "right now!" are essential for the system. In general, the more neurotic and stuck in their childhood, the more successful a consumer they are.

The physiological origins of the inconsistent and childish behaviors detected in neurotics, which were not seen in their past lives, can be clarified as follows. A small stimulus, which could have been quickly suppressed in previous lives, may cause the formation of foci of excitation in the cerebral cortex of people who have entered a vicious circle, who are, in a sense, 'exhausted,' and tend to become independent. Since the parts of the cerebral cortex that would balance these islets, whose excitement tension has increased to a high degree, are also kept under intense inhibition, these neurotic behavioral disruptions may emerge as 'oddities' that have been stripped of social values that were not seen in their past lives (Teber, 2018, p. 283). There is a need to sift through inhibition here. Humanity is experiencing a collective inhibition, as many frivolous topics are seriously discussed among people, and ignorance is increasing. Since the ego cannot support certain functions with the right stimuli from outside, it shuts down and locks some of its parts, which could lead to delayed maturation and continued infantilization. The fact that visual culture is far from formations and experiences that develop the cerebral cortex and that all kinds of information are superficialized and taken in without the need to think prevents the adequate development of the human cerebral cortex. Thus, as Teber puts it, on the one hand, the cerebral cortex is suppressed by boundary inhibition; on the other hand, the tension of the sub-cortical structures of the brain is increased. Under these conditions, these individuals often start acting on instinctive tendencies beyond the hitherto customary values. Therefore, neurotics may often display, for example, aggressive behavior, dietary and sexual desires, and lifestyle specialities (Teber, 2018, p. 284). Increased aggressive behaviors may only sometimes be at the level of physical actions at the legal level. They are directly reflected in speech under the influence of subconscious levels and can turn into a form that scratches the environment and the person. In fact, in some settings, all levels of speech can turn into this. Inhibition is the cause of this speech-enhancing situation.

If we accept that life determines consciousness, as Marx and Engels stated, we can say that postmodern life practices have evolved towards a fairytale structure. In a virtual culture, humanity is stuck in childhood. In his work *The Extinction of Childhood*, Neil Postman states that alphabetic culture and other means based on coding produce the concept of childhood because there was a time when human beings needed to learn codes. We have said that the difference between the child and adult worlds is opened by developing a culture based on symbolic coding. In ancient times, symbolic coding was not widespread. For example, in the Spartans, a child was subjected to military training from age 7 and became a soldier at age 20. In medieval societies, boys and girls could marry at an early age because there were no apparent differences between them and adults. There was also no need for a school-age to learn social experiences. Paul Virilio refers to this situation as "the disturbance of the developmental process leading to intellectual, sexual, sensory, psychomotor disorders, the lack of maturity of individuals trapped in their children." Virilio states that new technologies' weakening of the link between the real and the unreal is the main factor in creating a fairy tale environment. Subjects in society now seem to live in a fairy tale environment. They can turn into fairy tale heroes anytime through a television movie or a computer game.

In land-based societies, childhood is not as distinct as it is today; alphabetic culture has made childhood more and more distinct; visual culture will expand and universalize childhood. There is a growing disconnect between experience and material reality. People are exposed to this new type of experience very early. The "world of escape" creates a barrier between people and reality due to the suffering in class society. In addition, the urge to immediately fulfill a child's expectations is the dominant consumer culture today. In the future, this situation will gradually shift the gap between childhood and adulthood towards the side of childhood and create a new type of individual over time. Compared to modern times, today's children's identification with the myth of the individual from a very early age and their reactions to the rapid fulfillment of their expectations despite their delusions that they are individuals are examples that support these narratives.

It is well known that children's speech practices are grounded at an early age in the educational institutions of school and that school is where they learn the known moral patterns of society. School is a training camp before teaching. It is an institution where obedience, submission to authority, integration into the system by giving up one's existence, and the infinity of one's existence are imposed. The school is a center of self-existence massacre where all kinds of symbolic violence are experienced. Many faces of the pleasure of being in power and the alienation of power are experienced here. The school, where speech is regulated at an early age and where one meets the cultural structure required for integration into the system, is a center of subject education behind what it teaches.

As Ranciere emphasizes, the teacher-student relationship cannot be a "teaching" that flows from a "knowing" subject to people who do not know. Active teaching can only be possible with a "teacher" who accepts, recognizes, discusses, and allows the limitations of their knowledge to be discussed. As long as the relationship between someone who "knows" a lot and someone who "knows" little is a relationship of "seminar," which means bread, it is nothing but propaganda or, in Bourdieu's terms, symbolic violence. The theatre and humor played against all forms of symbolic violence, and the "you are right, sir" rituals to end the violence early are the tactics of the victim of violence to escape from the game.

Symbolic violence is hidden behind what is ostensibly accepted, familiar, and legitimized. In some areas, it develops behind the game's rules and becomes a stakeholder of alienation. In other spaces, what is perceived as harsh and violent is, on the contrary, a practice of protection. It is a necessity for the game in the field to protect the players and for the functionality to continue without harm.

Although the essence of the symbolic violence at school is extremely rude, and its outer surface appears very thin and naive, an example that is the opposite of this naivety and polite-looking communication can clarify what it means in countries like Turkey, where occupational safety is inferior and social living spaces, and dangerous work are co-located, harsh, rude and meaningless sounds emanating from construction sites. City dwellers who walk by these construction sites at high risk cannot make sense of these sounds; they are just rude noises to them. However, these sounds are a form of communication necessary for construction. They save energy in the face of impossibilities and contain commands that speed up the work. The release provided by shouting to the cortisone-laden bodies secreted by hours of intense and heavy work is an additional gain to all these narratives. The construction worker communicates with other coworkers meters away, pushes them to the action necessary for the work, and provides reassurance thanks to his shouting voice, which sometimes seems meaningless to those outside. The seeming violence in this communication embodies necessary acceptability. Because if they do not shout, crossing dangerous corridors endangers their lives. Bosses do not buy them walkie-talkies to earn more money. Communication in construction makes shouting and loud noises compulsory for occupational safety. Immediately after the violent phenomenon in the image in construction, the pleasant teas and sincere conversations during the break indicate this and relational normality. As can be seen, while the subtle and naïve language at school harbors a giant symbolic violence underneath, the forms of communication that appear much coarser and harsher when viewed from the outside contain a series of necessities that cannot be understood unless one gets involved.

The internet and television are the primary tools that determine public opinion and the dominant paradigm of society. There is no need to go into the history of television in this study; much has been written about it, but mentioning the infantilizing aspect of television can explain the domestication of speech. The means of communication have an impact on speech. Human beings experience the world in a spatially limited way. People are born in a particular area, especially if they are not born into the ruling classes, and no matter how nomadic they live, they can only move around a certain number of places. Like the medieval person, the child learns about the world from myths. These modern myths form their vocabulary of knowledge through school, the institution of religion, and the media. In pre-modern times, these myths were anonymous, but in modern times, these maps of meaning are presented to him by the mass media and the state apparatus. The subject is a poetic being and seeks to mean everywhere. This requirement of its nature continues today thanks to the internet and television, and the means of communication are at a point where they determine the topics of conversation.

The dominant electronic creators of public discourse cannot use the expressions used in language as diversely as a book. They spread messages with popular discourse without overtaxing the brain or providing in-depth information. It does not use too many words and metaphors; it simplifies the language. A minimum of talent and language skills are sufficient to decipher his messages. It is organized for below-average intelligence. Therefore, as in Orwell's "Newspeak" theory, it creates an audience that thinks in fewer and fewer words. Just like children, a society that thinks in fewer and fewer words is in the interest of the ruling classes.

According to Ivan Illich, the voices emitted by editors and presenters of programmed texts distort the meaning of words, turning spoken language into blocks of packaged messages. Today, for one's children to play in an environment where they will listen to people and not to stars, announcers, or educators, one must live in isolation, deprived of everything, or become a hippie, escaping to an affluent nature carefully protected from city life. The rapid encroachment of disciplined docility, the typical character of the spectator, the patient, and the client, can be observed worldwide. The standardization of human action is proliferating (Illich, 2010, p. 28). Moreover, social media and corporate television, which seem to have stepped out of this standardization, no matter how diverse they may appear in their outer shell, are, in essence, concerned with single propaganda—selling themselves to subjects. In doing so, it consumes clichéd and circulated words and carries new and meaningless words. This blow to the vocabulary of languages also damages the richness of people's intellectual world. Because language is thought, and thought is language.

More than fifty languages disappeared after the second half of the twentieth century; half of the languages still spoken in 1950 survive today only as the subject of doctoral dissertations. Languages that once witnessed incomparably different ways of seeing, using, and enjoying the world are now more similar (Illich, 2010, p. 31). Although it is not the only reason, the standardization of the means of communication has led to the atrophy of language and a different process of formation from its natural evolution over thousands of years.

Capitalization, also known as Westernization, has affected the languages of many countries, including Europe. However, most of all, it has affected the languages of third-world peoples and even destroyed some of them. This is because life practices influence language, and the technology developed by cultures that have capital due to colonization puts pressure on cultures that cannot develop this technology and are prevented from having it by various policies. At least this situation lasted until the 1970s when the locals gained value thanks to postmodern movements.

Commodities produced before the spread of the post Fordist mode of production were first used by the ruling classes. The language of these classes, especially in the colonial parts of the world, has been affected by Westernization much more than other classes. The native rulers of the colonial state grasped the language, lifestyle, and culture of the exploiters much faster. The fact that the bourgeois lifestyle much more influences them than other classes can be seen in the indicators in their language. However, over time, especially after the Second World War, as a result of the spread of petty-bourgeois culture almost all over the world and the gradual thinning of customs walls in non-central/peripheral countries after 1980, every class in society has fused with the languages of the cultures that have more capital and are active in the production of commodities. Even if this is a natural transformation throughout history, it has never happened so fast. This high speed brings problems of adaptation and unequal participation in world culture. For equal participation in world culture, cultures need to preserve their languages and participate in this equal participation with their mother tongues. However, this egalitarian structure is not possible in the current evolution of capitalism. This new chaotic structuring also significantly affects speech, one of the essential acts of human beings.

The Last Word

This study discusses the domestication and integration of speech into the system and the absorption of even fractured/different voices by this system. How should one respond to all these positionings? Schizoid and fragmatic, living in a state of constant revolutionary transformation, not knowing one's place, and being constantly displaced and stateless; perhaps this is the root of the answer and resistance. However, human beings cannot be homeless by their very nature because all primates define a territory and leave it only when faced with complex conditions. Without roots and place, there can be no language; without language, there can be no human being.

Therefore, speech and human consciousness are not independent of external reality and are phenomena directly constituted by reality. We have lived in a spoken universe with much more natural conditions for thousands of years than today. Geography and the isolation of human groups led to the separation and differentiation of spoken language and the formation of languages. During these thousands of years, language has been the home of human beings.

However, in modern times, the subject has been expelled from this house and dragged into a chaotic speech environment. The natural structure of speech has been disrupted, and the state's dominance over language has reached dimensions as terrifying as dystopian novels. After the liberalization of states, the brutal conditions of the free market shattered the meaning maps of speech and dealt a significant blow to the most critical human agency.

As a result of the change in external reality and the mass media in the second half of the twentieth century, and especially tools such as television and computers, which spread visual culture, occupying a large part of the individual's life, it is seen that the world of meaning that the word meets has regressed. Television has influenced literature, and the process of fictionalizing novels to resemble television is an example.

It is seen that the content of speech, the meanings conveyed through it, has gradually taken on a structure that does not make us question the reasons for life practices and depoliticizes the form and content of questioning. What is transmitted has a structure that prevents individuals from making sense of the world; it has a function that ensures the decline of enlightenment, justifies an obscurantist process, and accelerates this process. The system mechanizes all the practices of the individual, and this is also reflected in speech. This structure, which legitimizes the ruling classes' attitudes towards life and legitimizes all kinds of stereotypical thoughts, also equips individuals with stereotypical ideas and closes their ears to alternative thoughts. Ambition, selfishness, greed, insatiability for more power, and other deficiencies become people's general and legitimate character.

However, this situation will change with new social transformations in periods when the tension in the dialectical poles of the classes that make up society will increase, that is, in line with the weakening of the power of the rulers who do not have a homogeneous unity as a result of their struggle among themselves. More and more people are getting to know each other through new means of communication, and the practices of marginalization are becoming less frequent than in the past. This is a prolonged change, but more differences can now live together. These new transformations are certainly hoping for democratic practices.

For the ruling class, in other words, the corporations and the bourgeoisie, to maintain their power, there are many forms of government. In this sense, there is no difference between social democracy and fascism for the ruling economic class. However, there is a big difference for the people, and this difference is that democratic conditions must be put in place, especially when social democracy is in power. The way must be paved for free speech and scientific activities to be presented to the public. Power has changed, but perhaps one of the biggest problems for humanity is that the processes of transformation have become internalized, and totalitarianism has become abstract, infiltrating all the activities of the individual and turning it into a screw in the wheel, which is taken for granted and legitimized. For this reason, speech is a weapon when used freely for marginalized groups outside the ruling classes.

It is necessary to reflect on Jean-Paul Sartre's sentence, "I say 'no' because I am human," inspired by Descartes, and to see that perhaps the first condition that makes a human being human is to oppose the established order. Individuals are increasingly turning into the subjects that make up the societies found in science fiction scenarios and dystopias. However, dialectical materialism, one of the universe's fundamental laws, shows that the sovereignty of the sovereign can never dominate the entire society in a reified form and that an opposing force will be activated. Each of the seemingly opposing poles is composed of multiplicities, and those constitute life. Multiplicities cannot be controlled by any class or caste, no matter how much they try to control them. There will never be a power apparatus sophisticated enough to control the multitudes.

In this context, it would be an ethnocentric mistake to look at the diminishing capacity of speech to carry resistive meanings, i.e., the domestication of speech, and assume that all processes of history will continue in this way, and this would lead people to the mistake of declaring the "end of history." The change in material conditions and the transformation of society will equip the spoken word with resistive content when these transformation processes get stuck, and the dissemination of this spoken word will be able to reach much broader segments of society through new technologies.

References

Adorno, T. W. and Horkheimer, M. (2010). *Aydınlanmanın Diyalektiği [Dialectic of Enlightenment]*. Çev. Nihat Ünler, Elif Öztarhan Karadoğan. İstanbul: Kabalcı Yayınları.

Ağaoğulları, M. A. (2013). *Kent Devletinden İmparatorluğa [From City State to Empire]*. Ankara: İmge Kitabevi.

Akarsu, B. (1998). *Dil-Kültür Bağlantısı [Language-Culture Connectian]*. İstanbul: İnkılap Kitabevi.

Ateş, T. (2021). *Demokrasi [Democracy]*. Ankara: Ümit Yayıncılık.

Aytaç, G. (2005). *Edebiyat ve Kültür [Literature and Culture]*. Ankara: Hece Yayınları.

Bakan, J. (2007). *Şirket [Company]*. Çev. Rahmi G. Öğdül. İstanbul: Ayrıntı Yayınları.

Bakhtin, M. (2001). *Karnavaldan Romana [From Karnival To Novel]*. Çev. Sibel Irzık/ Cem Soydemir. İstanbul: Ayrıntı Yayınları.

Barthes, R. (2005). *Göstergebilimsel Serüven [The Semiotic Challenge]*. Çev. Mehmet Rıfat, Sema Rıfat. İstanbul: YKY.

Barthes, R. (1988). *Anlatıların Yapısal Çözümlemesine Giriş [Introduction to Structural Analysis of Narrative]*. Çev. Mehmet Rıfat, Sema Rıfat. İstanbul: Gerçek Yayınevi.

Baudrillard, J. (2005). *Şeytana Satılan Ruh ya da Kötülüğün Egemenliği [The Transparency of Evil: Essays on Extreme Phenomena]*. Çev. Oğuz Adanır. Ankara: Doğu Batı Yayınları.

Baudrillard, J. (2016). *Simülakrlar ve Simülasyon [Simulacra and Simulation]*. Çev. Oğuz Adanır, Ankara: Doğu Batı Yay.

Bauman, Z. (2022). *Kimlik [Identity]*. Çev. Mesut Hazır. Amkara: Heretik Yayınları.

Benton, T. and Craib, I. (2008). *Sosyal Bilim Felsefesi [Philosophy of Social Science]*. Çev. Ümit Tatlıcan, Berivan Binay. İstanbul: Sentez Yay.

Bernstein, B. (1999). *Popüler Kültür ve İktidar [Popular Culture and Power]*. Ankara: Vadi Yayınları.

Bewes, T. (2008). *Şeyleşme [Reification]*. Çev. Deniz Soysal. İstanbul: Metis Yayınları.

Biermann, W.; Klönne, A. (2007). *Kapitalizmin Suç Tarihi [The Criminal History of Capitalism]*. Çev. Bülent Özçelik. Ankara: Phoenix.

Blanchot, M. (1997). *İtiraf Edilemeyen Cemaat [The Unconfessed Community]*. Çev. Işık Ergüden. İstanbul: Ayrıntı Yayınları.

Blanchot, M. (2005). *Michel Foucault*. Çev. Ayşe Meral, İstanbul: Kabalcı Yayınevi.

Bourdieu, P. (2021). *Ayrım [Distinction]*. Çev. Derya Fırat, Günce Berkkurt. İstanbul: Nika Yayınevi.

Bourdieu, P. and Wacquant, L. (2014). *Düşünsel Bir Antropolojiye Doğru Cevaplar [Correct Answers to an Intellectual Anthropology]*. Çev. Nazlı Ökten. İstanbul: İletişim Yayınları.

Boyd, C. P. (2020). *Historia Patria: Politics, History, and National Identity in Spain, 1875-1975*. Princeton University Press.

Briggs, A. and Burke, P. (2021). *Medyanın Toplumsal Tarihi [Social History of Media]*. Çev. İbrahim Şener, İstanbul: İzdüşüm Yayınları.

Brooks, M. and Pickard, J. (2012). *Tarihsel Materyalizm ve Diyalektik Materyalizm [Historical Materialism and Dialectical Materialism]*. Çev. Hasan Erdem. İstanbul: Arya Yayıncılık.

Camus, A. (2012). *Yabancı [The Foreigner]*. Çev. Vedat Günyol. İstanbul: Can Yayınları.

Cassirer, E. (2005). *Kültür Bilimlerinin Mantığı Üzerine [On the Logic of Cultural Sciences]*. Çev. Milay Köktürk. Ankara: Hece Yayınları,

Charrier, J. P. (2020). *Bilinçdışı ve İnsan [Unconscious and Human]*. Çev. Hüsen Portakal, İstanbul: Cem Yayınevi.

Chul-Han, B. (2022a). *Erosun Istırabı [The Suffering of Eros]*. Çev. Şeyda Öztürk. İstanbul: Metis Yayınları.

Chul-Han, B. (2022b). *Şeffaflık Toplumu [Transparency Society]*. Çev. Haluk Barışcan. İstanbul: Metis Yayınları.

Cibran, H. (2021). *Aforizmalar [Aphorisms]*. Der. Orhan Düz, İstanbul: Avrupa Yakası Yayıncılık.

Cioran, E. M. (2012). *Çürümenin Kitabı [The Book of Decay]*. Çev. Haldun Bayrı. Metis Yayınları: İstanbul.

Clastres, P. (2016). *Devlete Karşı Toplum [Society versus State]*. Çev. Mehmet Sert, Nedim Demirtaş. İstanbul: Ayrıntı Yayınları.

Contat, M. (1996). *Sartre Sartre'ı Anlatıyor [Sartre Explains Sartre]*. Çev. Turhan Ilgaz. İstanbul: YKY.

Cowen, N. (2004). *Küresel Tarih [Global History]*. Çev. Cem Demirkan. İstanbul: Tümzamanlar Yay.

Crowley, D. and Heyer, P. (2017). *İletişim Tarihi [Contact Date]*. Çev. Berkay Ersöz. Ankara: İletişim Yayınları.

Cüceloğlu, D. (2020). *İnsan ve Davranışı [Human and Behavior]*, İstanbul: Remzi Kitabevi.

Dave, B. (2007). *Kazakhstan-Ethnicity, Language and Power*. Routledge.

Debord G. (2021). *Gösteri Toplumu [Society of the Spectacle]*, Çev: Ayşen Emekçi, Okşan Taşkent, İstanbul: Ayrıntı Yay.

Deleuze, G. (2020). *Anlamın Mantığı [Logic of Sense]*. Çev. Hakan Yücefer. İstanbul: Norgunk Yayıncılık.

Deleuze, G. (2023). *İktidar [Power]*. Çev. Sinem Özer, Münevver Çeliki, İstanbul: Otonom Yayıncılık.

Derrida, J. (2020). *Konukseverlik Üstüne [Of Hospitality]*. Çev. Aslı Sümer. İstanbul: Metis Yayınları.

Dwyer, John C. (1998). *Church History: Twenty Centuries of Catholic Christianity.* Mahwah, USA.: Paulist Press.

Edgar, A. L. (2006). *Tribal Nation: The Making of Soviet Turkmenistan.* Princeton University Press.

Ellul, J. (2004). *Sözün Düşüşü [The Fall of the Word].* Çev. Hüsamettin Arslan, İstanbul: Paradigma.

Evans-Pritchard, E. E. (1986). *The Nuer.* London: Oxford Press.

Fiske, J. (2009). *Mitler ve Mitleri Yapanlar [Myths and Myth Makers].* Çev. Şebnem Duran. İzmir: İlya Yayınevi.

Fitch, W. T. (2005). "The Evolution of Language: A Comparative Review", *Biology and Philosophy,* 20 (2-3), 193-203.

Foucault, M. (2003). *Cinselliğin Tarihi [History of Sexuality].* Çev. Hülya Uğur Tanrıöver. İstanbul: Ayrıntı Yayınları.

Foucault, M. (2006). *Kliniğin Doğuşu. [Birth of the Clinic].* Çev. İnci Malak Uysal, Ankara: Epos.

Foucault, M. (2019). *Hapishanenin Doğuşu [Discipline and Punish: The Birth of the Prison].* Çev. Mehmet Ali Kılıçbay. Ankara: İmge Kitabevi Yayınları.

Gerovitch, S. (2004). *From Newspeak to Cyberspeak: A History of Soviet Cybernetics.* Mit Press.

Giddens, A. (2021). *Kapitalizm ve Modern Sosyal Teori [Capitalism and Modern Social Theory].* Çev. Ümit Tatlıcan. İstanbul: İletişim Yayınları.

Girard, R. (2019). *Şiddet ve Kutsal [Violence and the Sacred].* Çev. Necmiye Alpay. İstanbul: Alfa Yayınları.

Gorz, A. (2022). *Maddesiz [Without Substance].* Çev. Işık Ergüden. İstanbul: Ayrıntı Yayınları.

Gürel, K. T. (2023). *Basında Homofobinin İnşası [Construction of Homophobia in the Press].* Çanakkale: Paradigma Akademi Yayınları.

Hacıkadiroğlu, V. (2002). *Özgürlük Hukuku [Freedom Law].* İstanbul: Cem Yayınevi.

Han, B. C. (2023). *Ritüellerin Yokoluşuna Dair [On the Disappearance of Rituals].* Çev. Çağlar Tanyeri, İstanbul: İnka Kitap.

Hançerlioğlu, O. (1977). *Özgürlük Düşüncesi [Thought of Freedom].* İstanbul: Varlık Yayınları.

Harari, Y. N. (2015). *Sapiens: A Brief History of Humankind.* New York: Vintage Publisher.

Hardt M. ve Negri A. (2011a). *Çokluk: İmparatorluk Çağında Savaş ve Demokrasi [Multitude: War and Democracy in the Age of Empire].* İstanbul: Ayrıntı Yayınları.

Hardt, M. and Negri, A. (2003). *İmparatorluk [Empire].* Çev. Abdullah Yılmaz. İstanbul: Ayrıntı Yayınları.

Hardt, M. and Negri, A. (2011b). *Ortak Zenginlik [Common Wealth].* Çev. Efla-Barış Yıldırım, İstanbul: Ayrıntı Yayınları.

Horkheimer, M. (2005). *Akıl Tutulması [Eclipse of Mind].* Çev. Orhan Koçak. İstanbul: Ayrıntı Yayınları.

Hunt-Jackson, J. L. (2007). *Finding Fathers' Voices: Exploring Life Experiences of Fathers of Children with Autistic Spectrum Disorders*. State University of New York at Buffalo.

Hyppolite, J. (1997). *Logic and Existence*. New York: Suny.

Ilin, M. and Segal E, (2016). *İnsan Nasıl İnsan Oldu? [How Man Became Human]*. Çev. Ahmet Zekerya. İstanbul: Say Yayınları.

Illich, I. (2010). *İşsizlik Hakkı [Unemployment Right]*. Çev. Deniz Keskin. İstranbul: Yeni İnsan Yayınevi.

İnal, Ayşe (2010). "Anlatı Yapıları ve Televizyonun Anlatısal Potansiyeli Üzerine Bir Tartışma", *Medyadan Söylemler*, Der. T. Durna., İstanbul: Libra Kitap, s. 19-45.

Irigaray, L. (2006). *Ben, Sen ve Biz [I, You and Us]*. Çev. Sabri Büyükdüvenci, Nilgün Tutal. İstanbul: İmge Kitabevi.

Irigaray, L. (2021). *Doğmak- Yeni İnsanın Başlangıcı [Being Born - The Beginning of a New Man]*. Çev. Naciye Sağlam. Ankara: Fol Kitap.

Jaspers, K. (2003). *Felsefi İnanç [Philosophical Belief]*. Çev. Akın Kanat, İzmir, İlya Yayınevi.

Jowett, G. S. and O'Donnell V. (2002). *Propaganda and Persuasion*. London: Sage Publications.

Jung, C. G. (2022). *İnsan Ruhuna Yöneliş [Man and His Symbols]*. Çev. Engin Büyükinal. İstanbul: Say Yayınları.

Karabey, H. (2001). *Sessiz Ölüm [Silent Death]*. İstanbul: Metis Yayınları.

Kellner, D. (2020). *Medya Gösterisi [Media Show]*. Çev. Zeynep Paşalı. İstanbul: Açılım Kitap.

Kerimoğlu, C. (2022). *Neanderthaller Konuşur Muydu? [Did Neanderthals Talk?]*. İzmir: Varyant Yayınları.

Köker, E. (2007). *Politikanın İletişimi İletişimin Politikası [Communication of Policy Policy of Communication]*. Ankara: İmge Kitabevi.

Kottak C. P. (2008). *Antropoloji [Anthropology]*. Çev. Sibel Özbudun. Ankara: Ütopya.

Kropotkin, P. (2001). *Karşılıklı Yardımlaşma [Mutual Aid]*. Çev. Işın Ergüden, Deniz Güneri. İstanbul: Kaos Yayınları.

L'Heuillet, H. (2022). *Gecikmeye Övgü [Praise for Delay]*. Çev. Şehsuvar Aktaş. İstanbul: Ayrıntı Yayınları.

Le Bon, G. (2009). *Kitleler Psikolojisi [Mass Psychology]*. Ankara: Alter Yayınları.

Leakey, R. (1993). *İnsanın Kökeni [The Origin of Humankind]*. Çev. Sinem Gül. İstanbul: Varlık Yayınları.

Lefebvre, H. (1998). *Modern Dünyada Gündelik Hayat [Everyday Life in the Modern World]*. Çev. Işın Gürbüz. İstanbul: Metis Yayınları.

Levi-Strauss, C. (1974). *Structural Anthropology, Translated by Claire Jacobson and Brooke Grundfest Schoepf*. New York: Basic Books.

Levi-Strauss, C. (1997). *Irk, Tarih ve Kültür [Race, History and Culture]*. Çev. Haldun Bayrı, Reha Erdem, Arzu Oyacıoğlu, Işık Ergüden. İstanbul: Metis Yayınları.

Lewin, R. (2004). *Human Evolution: An Illustrated Introduction.* New Jersey: John Wiley & Sons.

Lingis, A. (1997). *Ortak Bir Şeyleri Olmayanların Ortaklığı [Partnership of Those Who Have Nothing in Common].* Çev. Tuncay Birkan. İstanbul: Ayrıntı Yayınları.

Mannoni, P. (2009). *Korku [Fear].* Çev. Işın Gürbüz, İstanbul: İletişim Yayınları.

Martin, H. P. and Schumann, H. (2007). *Globalleşme Tuzağı [Globalization Trap].* Çev. Özden Saatçi Karadana, Mahmure Kahraman. Ankara: Ümit Yayıncılık.

Marx K. (2004a). *Alman İdeolojisi [German Ideology].* Çev. Sevim Belli. Ankara: Sol Yayınları.

Marx, K. (2004b). *Kapital [Capital].* I. Cilt, Çev. Alattin Bilgi. Ankara: Sol Yayınları.

Marx, K. (2007). Yabancılaşma *[Estrangement].* Der. Barışta Erdost, Çev. Sevim Belli. İstanbul: Sol Yayınları.

Maspul, K. A. (2022). "Coffee Acculturation in Saudi Arabia: Diversifying Local Wisdom and Strengthening Sustainable Economy in Coffee Value Chain". *EKOMA: Jurnal Ekonomi, Manajemen, Akuntansi,* 1 (2), 271-283.

McLuhan, M., and Fiore, Q. (2001). *Medium is The Message,* Ginko Press.

Mithen S. (2000). *Aklın Tarih Öncesi [Prehistory of the Mind].* Çev. İrem Kutluk. Ankara: Dost.

Morgan, L. H. (1986). *Eski Toplum-1 [Old Society- 1].* Çev. Ünsal Oskay. İstanbul: İnkılap Kitabevi.

Naz, N. (1997). *Baudelaire Efsanesi [The Legend of Baudelaire].* Ankara: X Yayınları.

Nevins, N. and Commager, H. S. (2005). *ABD Tarihi* [US History]. Çev. Halil İnalcık. Ankara: Doğu Batı Yayınları.

Nietzsche, F. (2009). *Ecce Homo,* Çev. Elif Yıldırım. İstanbul: Oda Yayınları.

Nietzsche, F. (2013). *Böyle Buyurdu Zerdüşt [Thus Spoke Zarathustra].* Çev. Mustafa Tüzel. İstanbul: Say Yayınları.

Nietzsche, F. (2022). *Gezgin ile Gölgesi [The Traveler and His Shadow].* Çev. İsmet Zeki Eyuboğlu. İstanbul: Broy Yayınları.

Orwell, G. (1999). *Bin Dokuz Yüz Seksen Dört [One Thousand Nine Hundred Eighty Four].* Çev. Nuran Akögren. İstanbul: Can Yayınları.

Özbek, M. (2000). *Dünden Bugüne İnsan [Human from Past to Present].* Ankara: İmge Kitabevi.

Özbudun, S. and Uysal, G. and Wilkinson-Duran, N. (1998). *İnsan: Doğası, Tarihöncesi, Kültürü [Man: Nature, Prehistory, Culture].* Ankara: Öteki Yayınevi.

Payne, S. G. (2011). *The Franco Regime, 1936–1975.* University of Wisconsin Press.

Pei, M. A. (1960). *The Story of Language.* Signet.

Ponting, C. (2012). *Dünyanın Yeşil Tarihi [Green History of the World].* Çev. Ayşe Başcı Sander. İstanbul: Sabancı Üniversitesi Yayınları.

Postman, N. (1995). *Çocukluğun Yokoluşu [The Disappearance of Childhood].* Çev. Kemal İnal, Ankara: İmge Yayınları.

Poulantzas, N. (1975). *Classes in Contemporary Capitalism*. NLB.

Revel, J. (2006). *Michel Foucault*. Çev. Kemal Atakay. İstanbul: Ayrıntı Yayınları.

Rıfat, M. (1990). *Dilbilim ve Göstergebilimin Çağdaş Kuramları [Contemporary Theories of Linguistics and Semiotics]*. İstanbul: Düzlem Yayınları.

Rifkin, J. (2001). *The Age of Access: The New Culture of Hypercapitalism*. Penguin.

Rosengren, K. E. (2008). *Communication*. London: Sage Publications.

Rousseau, J. J. (1998). *Bilimler ve Sanatlar Üstüne Söylev [Discourse on the Sciences and Arts]*. Çev. Sabahattin Eyuboğlu. İstanbul: Türkiye İş Bankası Yayınları.

Rousseau, J. J. (2019). *Toplum Sözleşmesi [Social Contract]*. Çev. Vedat Günyol. İstanbul: Türkiye İş Bankası Yayınları.

Sahlins, M. (2019). *Batı'nın İnsan Doğası Yanılsaması* [The West's Illusion of Human Nature]. Çev. Emine Ayhan, Zeynep Demirsü. İstanbul: BGST Yayınları.

Sarup, M. (1997). *Post-Yapısalcılık ve Postmodernizm [Post-Structuralism and Postmodernism]*. Çev. A. Baki Güçlü. Ankara: Ark.

Schiller, H. (2022). *Zihin Yönlendirenler [Mind Manipulators]*. Çev. Cevdet Cerit. İstanbul: Pınar Yayınları.

Schor, J. (1991). *The Overworked American*. New York: Basic Books.

Şenel, A. (2009). *İnsanlık Tarihi [Human History]*. Ankara: İmge Kitabevi.

Shepard, T. (2006). *The Invention of Decolonization: The Algerian War and The Remaking of France*. Cornell University Press.

Sombart, W. (1998). *Aşk, Lüks ve Kapitalizm [Love, Luxury and Capitalism]*. Çev. Necati Aça. Ankara: Bilim ve Sanat.

Sontag, S. (1999). *Fotoğraf Üzerine [On Photography]*. Çev. Reha Akçakaya. İstanbul: Altıkırkbeş Yayınları.

Spiteri, E.; Konopka, G.; Coppola, G.; Bomar, J.; Oldham, M.; Ou, J.; et al. (2007). "Identification of the Transcriptional Targets of FOXP2, A Gene Linked to Speech and Language, in Developing Human Brain", *The American Journal of Human Genetics*, 81 (6), 1144-1157.

Spolsky, B. (2004). *Language Policy*. Cambridge University Press.

Squatriti, P. (2014). "Pornocracy", In Christopher Kleinhenz (Ed.), Medieval Italy: An Encyclopedia, Vol. 2. New York and London: Routledge.

Stokoe, W. C. (1978). "Sign Language Versus Spoken Language", *Sign Language Studies*, 69-90.

Taddei, A. (2017). *Hagia Sophia before Hagia Sophia*. A study of the Great Church of Constantinople from its origins to the Nika Revolt of 532. Campisano Editore Srl.

Teber, S. (2004). *Davranışlarımızın Kökeni [The Origin of Our Behavior]*. İstanbul: Say Yayınları.

Teber, S. (2018). *İlk Toplumların Değişimleri [Changes of the First Societies]*. İstanbul: Say Yayınevi.

Thompson, J. B. (2008). *Medya ve Modernite [Media and Modernity]*. Çev. Serdar Öztürk. İstanbul: Kırmızı Yayınları.

Todorov, T. (2008). *Ortak Hayat [Common Life]*. Çev. Mehmet Emin Özcan. Ankara: Dost Yayınları.

Topbaş, O. N. (2005). *Abı Hayat Katreleri [Drops of Water of Immortality]*. Ankara: Erkam Yayınları.

Tubbs, S. L. and Moss, S. (2003). *Human Communication*. New York: Mc. Graw Hill Companies.

Veblen, T. (2005). *Aylak Sınıfın Teorisi [Theory of the Leisure Class]*. Çev. Cumhur Atay. İstanbul: Babil Yayınları.

Virilio, P. (2021). *Enformasyon Bombası [Information Bomb]*. Çev. Kaya Şahin. İstanbul: Metis Yayınları.

Volaşinov, V. N. (2001). *Marksizm ve Dil Felsefesi [Marxism and Philosophy of Language]*. Çev. Mehmet Küçük. İstanbul: Ayrıntı Yayınları.

Weber, M. (2008). *Sosyoloji Yazıları [Sociology Articles]*. Çev. Taha Parla. İstanbul: Deniz Yayınları.

Wright, S. (2016). *Language Policy and Language Planning: From Nationalism to Globalisation*. Springer.

Zamyatin, Y. İ. (2019). *Biz [Us]*. Çev. Serdar Arıkan. İstanbul: İthaki Yayınları.

Zerzan, J. (2004). *Gelecekteki İlkel [Future Primitive]*. Çev. Cemal Atila. İstanbul: Kaos Yayınları.

Zijderveld, A. C. (2022). *Sahnelik Toplum [Stage Society]*. Çev. Kadir Canatan. İstanbul: Pınar Yayınları.

Zizek, S. (2019). *İdeolojinin Yüce Nesnesi [The Supreme Object of Ideology]*. Çev. Tıncay Birkan. İstanbul: Metis Yayınları.

Zubritski, Mitropolski, Kerov (2012). *İlkel, Köleci ve Feodal Toplum [Primitive, Slave and Feudal Society]*. Çev. Sevim Belli. Ankara: Sol Yayınları.

Index

68, 77, 91, 93, 103, 106, 107, 109,
111, 113
monarchy, 35
mother tongues, 37, 112
mythology, 5, 79

N

Neanderthal, 3, 7, 11, 12, 13
neoliberalism, 34
Newspeak, 87, 88, 111
non-linguistic, 79

P

Paleolithic, 9, 13, 24
parliamentary, 39
patriarchal, 4, 77
perpetrator, 58, 80
phantasmatic supports, 59
phenomenon, 14, 23, 27, 29, 38,
42, 43, 44, 50, 51, 52, 55, 60, 84,
99, 111
Populism, 50
pornocracy, 102
post Fordist, xiii, 39, 40, 43, 59, 62,
99
postmodern, 31, 39, 40, 41, 55, 60,
62, 64, 66, 67, 68, 76, 83, 84, 85,
86, 92, 93, 94, 109, 112
Power, 13, 16, 20, 22, 23, 24, 25, 26,
27, 30, 32, 33, 40, 42, 44, 45, 48,
49, 50, 51, 53, 54, 55, 56, 57, 58,
60, 62, 63, 64, 65, 66, 69, 73, 77,
80, 81, 83, 85, 88, 89, 90, 91, 93,
94, 95, 99, 100, 105, 107, 110, 114
praxis, 120
Prayer, 19, 22, 26
prison, 5, 34, 35, 45, 47, 48, 50, 60,
62, 63, 64, 65, 66, 67
propaganda, 6, 34, 94, 100, 105,
107, 110, 112

punishment, 52, 54, 55, 56, 57, 59,
62, 63, 64, 66

R

radio, 27, 43, 96, 98, 99, 100, 101
rituals, 16, 17, 19, 22, 32, 33, 36, 93,
103
Revolution, 7, 21, 34, 35, 40, 59, 80,
83, 92, 93, 94, 101, 105, 107, 113

S

Saphir-Whorf hypothesis, 8
selfishness, 114
sexual, 2, 77, 86, 109
shaman, 19
signifier, 13, 56, 74, 91, 92, 104,
sign, 3, 13, 17, 19, 27, 45, 51, 53, 64,
70, 71, 75, 78, 86, 89, 90, 91, 92,
98, 101, 103, 105, 106
slavery, 26, 34, 83, 99
Socialism, 35
sonic capital, 27
state, 2, 4, 9, 11, 15, 19, 21, 22, 23,
24, 26, 29, 30, 34, 35, 36, 37, 38,
39, 40, 43, 44, 45, 49, 52, 53, 54,
55, 57, 59, 60, 65, 66, 67, 69, 70,
76, 79, 81, 89, 90, 92, 94, 96, 97,
98, 101, 102, 103, 111, 112, 113
Stone Age, 10, 11, 13
storyteller, 33
surveillance society, 53
symbolic violence, 34, 36, 44, 110,
111

T

Telephone, 93, 96, 97, 98, 99
Tower of Babel, 84, 85
transmission, 11, 14, 42, 55, 86, 87,
96